Bible FUNS

CHILDREN'S SERMONS

in a Bag

WRITTEN BY

MARY GRACE BECKER

CHILDREN'S SERMONS IN A BAG
Published by David C. Cook
4050 Lee Vance View
Colorado Springs, CO 80918 U.S.A.

David C. Cook Distribution Canada
55 Woodslee Avenue, Paris, Ontario, Canada N3L 3E5

David C. Cook U.K., Kingsway Communications
Eastbourne, East Sussex BN23 6NT, England

David C. Cook and the graphic circle C logo are registered trademarks of Cook Communications
Ministries.

Written by Mary Grace Becker
Cover Design: Peter Schmidt and Scot McDonald, Granite Design
Interior Design: Dana Sherrer, iDesignEtc.

Scripture quotations, unless otherwise noted, are taken from the Holy Bible, NEW INTERNATIONAL
READER'S VERSION©. Copyright© 1996, 1998 International Bible Society. All rights reserved throughout
the world. Used by permission of International Bible Society.

ISBN 978-0-7814-3958-9

First Printing 2003
Printed in the United States

3 4 5 6 7 8 9 10 11 12
122007

Table of Contents

SEASONAL SERMONS

Introduction

Adam and Eve were created from an apple tree.
Noah's wife was called Joan of Ark.
Noah built an ark, and the animals came in pears.

You can never be sure what you're going to hear in the middle of a children's sermon. The spontaneous interaction with kids is part of what makes a children's sermon delightful to give—and for the congregation to hear. And they *are* listening!

Children's Sermons in a Bag is a celebration of how children learn—through wiggling and responding to what's around them and feeling with their whole bodies—and the belief that God, through his Word, wants to transform children from simple earth-bound beings to spiritual ones alive in him. Child development and spiritual formation are not two separate, unconnected issues, but ones that work together to open a child's heart to the awesomeness of God. Undeniably, his touch changes lives.

My dog doesn't want my broccoli either.

God has spoken in his Word through story. Seek and you shall find joy! Through Bible stories and key verses children come to understand the joyful, loving and trustworthy character of God. Today's sermons encourage participation, heighten enthusiasm and, most importantly, increase the spiritual development of your children on their lifelong journey toward the Son. The sermons in this book are organized around the themes of "God Loves Me," "I Love God" and "I Love Others." The last section offers a selection of talks for specific seasons, such as Christmas, Easter and Pentecost.

Imagination plays a vital role as children stretch to understand the stories of the Bible and God's involvement in their lives. See in the pages that follow how to embrace imagination; after all, the power of forming images of reality in children's minds is a gift of God. Help kids put their imaginations to work to learn to know God better. S-t-r-e-t-c-h!

Sleep in heavenly peas . . .

To get started you'll need your Bible and a "grab bag." A "grab bag" can be whatever you wish. A simple grocery sack will work, or mix it up from week to week—a backpack one week and luggage-on-wheels the next. Or the all-mysterious shopping bag may be just the thing to entice the curiosity of your children. Each week you'll fill the grab bag with a few simple supplies. Be sure to read over the sermon a few days before presentation. You may need to make copies of a reproducible and spend a few minutes cutting and coloring.

What color is a hiccup?

Do you have lots of preschoolers in your church? Use the well-crafted methods provided here, but keep an ever-watchful eye on little ones. Beads, balloons, small toys, even plastic cups and paper can be choking hazards for small children. Members of your congregation will be more than happy to be your volunteer "eyes." Or simply demonstrate the activity and have children give it a try at home with Mom and Dad.

What's pink and gray and has four feet?
A hippopotamus sticking its tongue out.

Ready? Get set. Relax! You're not alone. Trust that God will work through you in spite of the interruptions, cries and false starts that are sure to be a part of any children's talk. Relax! God will find the way that works for your children to discover that they are precious and irreplaceable in his sight. Relax! Notice that all the sermons end on a quiet reflective note. Allow this brief prayer time to bring your children together in prayerful worship.

Where does the sun go at night?

Lastly, many sermons have the congregation in mind as well as the kids. Watch as moms, dads, grandmas and grandpas anticipate the joy to come: children absorbed in the discovery of a Bible truth. Use this relaxed and happy time to encourage the entire church community to see themselves and God in the way that God intends.

How much do you love Jesus? Show me!

Beep! Time to turn the page and get started!
You're ready to leave God's imprint on the lives of those who seek to love him.

Mary Grace Becker

God Loves Me!

It's a plain fact: children need love to thrive. And there is no better love than God's love. The children's sermons in this section will help you share the wonder and security that come with reveling in God's love. God wants the best for us, and he gives us what we need for every situation. Do we need strength? Our loving God gives it. Do we need wisdom? Our loving God gives it. Do we wonder about the future? Our loving God is in control of it. Help your kids celebrate: God loves me!

Thankful Rub-a-dub Tub

On Your Mark

Bible Truth: God wants the best for us.

Bible Verse: May the LORD bless you and take good care of you. May the LORD smile on you and be gracious to you. May the LORD look on you with favor and give you his peace (Numbers 6:24–26).

Godprint: Preciousness

Get Set

Grab Bag: Bible, a freezer zip-top bag (fill it 1/2 full with blue or green hair gel and a dash of glitter, then seal), a roll or bag of new pennies, a new shower curtain for your children to sit on, wet wipes for sticky fingers. Optional: a rubber ducky, a shower cap

GO!

Spread out the shower curtain and have children sit on it. Reach into your grab bag and pull out the shower cap and put it on. **Can I see a shower of happy smiles to start our time together?**

• Who takes care of you the moment you jump out of bed in the morning?
• How does a smile from someone you love make you feel hopeful and happy inside?

A warm shower or bath feels wonderful on a chilly morning. Reach into your grab bag and pull out the rubber ducky. Give it a squeeze. **And since I didn't bring my bathtub with me, I have the next best thing.** Reach into your grab bag again and pull out the zip-top gel bag. **A bath in a bag!** Place the bag on the floor in front on you. Allow children to feel the shiny smooth surface. **Look at all the bubbles!**

In today's Bible verse we hear something that God said to Moses. God's people, the Israelites, were wandering around the desert. God loved his people very much, and he wanted the priests to give the people a special blessing to let them know God wanted the best for them. Blessings meant only good things, happy things, as well as God's help when the people needed it most. God wanted his people to have a "blessing bath!" Today we're going to help some of God's people take a blessing bath.

• What happy blessings does God give you?

Read Numbers 6:24-26. **Scrub a dub tub! God wants his people to be happy and well taken care of. Let's drop some of God's people into the tub!** Reach into your grab bag and pull out your roll or bag of pennies. Have a helper distribute one penny each to four or five children. Caution: Pennies are choking hazards for young children. Allow young children to accept a penny and then drop it immediately into the gel bag under your supervision.

Scrub a dub tub! God also wants his people to do what pleases him. Then the Lord smiles on us to let us know he's happy about the choices we're making. Let's drop more of God's people into the tub! Distribute more pennies and have the children drop them into the bag.

Scrub a dub tub! God wants his people to have peace—a peace so special that it can only come from him. Drop God's people into the tub! Distribute the rest of the pennies and watch as they drop into the bag. **We're safe in a shower of God's blessings.**

• Tell me something that makes you feel peaceful.
• Why do you think God wants his people to have peace?

What a wonderful and warm place to be—bathed and blessed in the love of God. It's so great to know that God loves us and wants the best for us. Seal the bag and have children push the "Israelites" in and around the blessings of God.

After a while put the bag away and gather to pray. **Dear God, thank you for the wonderful gift of you! Bless us so we may be a blessing to others. In Jesus' name, amen.**

Armor All

On Your Mark

Bible Truth: God gives us what we need to stand up against evil.

Bible Story: Armor of God, Ephesians 6:10–18

Godprint: Courage

Get Set

Grab Bag: Bible, sports bag filled with a variety of sports equipment: football helmet, elbow pads; baseball cap, jersey, cleats; hockey gloves or skates; soccer or volley ball; tennis racquet; goggles; snorkel; golf club, etc.

GO!

I'm all set for a fun game of bowling. I just love picking up the ball, putting just the right spin on it and watching it—smash!—into the pins. Point to the bag by your side. **I'll need some volunteer helpers to help me get ready for the big game.** Pause as your volunteers join you. **Please reach into my grab bag and pull out one item. Then you can help me put it on.** Get to it! Keep dressing and layering sports equipment until the sports bag is empty. Thank your volunteers and have them sit down again.

There! I'm all ready to score a perfect 300 game! Stand up so the congregation can get the full effect! **Give me a thumbs up or down to show if you like my choices.**

• Do I have everything I need to go bowling? *(Listen to your children's responses.)*
• How does the right equipment help protect a sports team from injury?

Sit down. **So what I hear you saying is I have a lot of stuff, but I don't have what I need to get the job done.** Take off all the equipment and read Ephesians 6:10, 11 from your Bible or ask a volunteer to read.

• What's the big job we need to do in these verses? *(Fight the devil.)*
• What does God give us to help us do this job? *(God's armor.)*

Hmm. I see now that I'm not prepared, even if I think I am, to play the game to win. It's the same way in real life. God tells us it's not enough to fight off the devil with our own strength. We need the right equipment—God's brand of armor. Who'd like to read all the pieces of armor our loving God provides?

Hand the Bible to a child to read Ephesians 6:13–18 or have several children take turns, one verse each. **Because God gives us what we need, we can stand up against evil.**

• What pieces of God's armor did you hear in these verses?
• Who is our enemy? What is he trying to do?
• When have you needed God's help to walk away from something you knew was wrong?
• When should we pray for God's help? *(At all times.)*

Let's pray in the Spirit now with our prayers and requests. Pause for prayer. **Dear God, we are stronger with you than we can ever be on our own. Help us stay well protected against the devil's harmful ways. Amen!**

Remember that God loves each of you times two! Make a cross with two fingers. **Not only will he supply you with armor, but also every morning he'll help you put it on. Pray and allow God to do this for you.** Point to your mismatched collection of equipment. **Unlike me, God won't get it all mixed up! His armor is the perfect fit and perfectly suited to shoo the devil far, far away.**

Cruise Line

On Your Mark

Bible Truth: God takes care of us in any situation.

Bible Story: Noah, Genesis 6:5–19

Godprint: Trust

Get Set

Grab Bag: Bible, big furry slippers (bunnies, if you have them!). Optional: a portable CD player with upbeat marching music and a big bag of stuffed animals, one per child

GO!

Reach into your grab bag for your bunny slippers and step into them. **I'm sure you all know the Bible story of Noah and the very special boat he built called the ark. I'll just relax here while you tell me all about it!** Pause and listen to your children tell the story of Noah.

Yes, lots of animals found a home on the big boat Noah and his sons built. But let's back up a bit now and find out why God asked Noah to build the ark. Open your Bible and read Genesis 6:5–7 or ask a good reader to help.

• How does it feel when your heart hurts?
• What do these Bible verses say was making God's heart hurt? *(The evil on the earth.)*

Read Genesis 6:8. **Noah was a very good man in a very bad place. People on earth no longer listened to God or obeyed his commandments. They lied and used angry fists to solve their problems. They were selfish and disobedient—much like people today. But Noah walked with God and knew right from wrong. And God loved him and kept him safe when the flood came.**

Finish by reading Genesis 6:9–19.

• God cares for animals! What's your favorite?
• How do you think Noah was feeling when it started raining? How about 40 days later?

Let's name a few of the animals that marched into the ark two by two. Pause as children mention birds, hamsters, dogs, cats, camels, cows, canaries and koalas!

Who else went aboard the ark to escape the floodwaters? Pause. Of course! Noah and his family! Noah trusted God to take care of him in any situation, and God did. You can trust God too. He'll take care of you.

Stand and address your congregation. **Ladies and gentlemen, we need an ark! Can I have some help from our moms and dads?**

Have volunteers stand up and form two lines facing each other. If you have a center aisle, they could stand in the aisle.

Let's make an ark for your children. Raise your hands and join them across the way. Good! Head back to your kids and turn on the happy marching music from the CD. **Sounds like our marching orders are in. It's time to cruise on down the line and into the ark—just like Noah and his family.**

Invite children to follow you as you march into the ark to the encouraging cheers of parents. If you have a big bag of stuffed animals, have kids grab one before they enter the ark. After all the children exit the ark, say, …**and just like Noah, God takes us safely to higher ground!** If time permits, have children circle the church for a second go 'round before joining their parents and returning to their seats.

Happy Meal

On Your Mark

Bible Truth: God gives us what we need; we can be thankful.

Bible Verse: When the dew was gone, thin flakes appeared on the desert floor. They looked like frost on the ground. The people of Israel saw the flakes. They asked each other, "What's that?'"They didn't know what it was. Moses said to them, "It's the bread the LORD has given you to eat" (Exodus 16:14, 15).

Godprint: Thankfulness

Get Set

Grab Bag: Bible, cereal box, a favorite camping shirt or hat, a little stuffed bear

Ahead of time, remove the bagged cereal from inside the box and replace it with a bag of round vanilla wafers.

GO!

Who enjoys camping in the great outdoors with their families?

- What's your favorite camping food?
- Which meal do you like best…breakfast, lunch or dinner?

Reach into your grab bag and pull out your favorite camping shirt and put it on. **It's been a fabulous day camping here in** (fill in the name of your church)_____ **Campground. But now it's bedtime.** Yawn and stretch. **How do I know?** Take a deep breath. **The stars sparkle overhead and the air smells like burnt marshmallows!** Fold your hands, prayerlike, and press them to your cheek. Have the children follow your lead.

Soon…we…are…peacefully…asleep. Close your eyes and snore—loudly! ZZZZZZZZ. After a few seconds open your eyes. **Good morning, everyone. I'm hungry. How do scrambled eggs, flapjacks, sizzling bacon and fresh jelly doughnuts sound?**

Open your grab bag and take a look inside. Then shake your head. **Uh oh. Our breakfast is on hold this morning.** Reach into your grab bag and pretend to struggle with it. Then gently pull out the little stuffed bear. **Sometime in the middle of the night a bear caught a whiff of our food**

bag. Ms. Bear helped herself to all of our breakfast fixings. What shall we do now? *(A likely response from your children: Get in the car and head for a favorite local pancake house!)*

Great idea! But the Israelites in today's Scripture had no way to get to a restaurant or a convenience store. They were stuck in the middle of a great desert and needed to rely on God to provide their breakfast. Open your Bible and read Exodus 16:14, 15.

• What did God give the people in this story?

The people needed food, so God gave them food. He gave them just what they needed. The people called this food "manna," and God sent manna every morning.

Reach into your grab bag and take out the box of "cereal." **Breakfast of camp-ions!** Open it and let your children help themselves to the wafers. **Wafers of honey made an excellent low-fat happy meal for God's hungry children.** Pat the stuffed bear and place her back in the grab bag. **But, by all means, keep them away from the bears!**

Mmm. I wonder what else the people needed.

Have a reader read Exodus 17:5, 6.

• What did God give the people this time?

God even provided the beverage! Yum! That was good. Whatever our bodies need, God knows what to shop for. Let's be thankful that God gives us what we need.

Bow heads in prayer. **Dear God, when tummies rumble and grumble, we're thankful for the food you provide. Help us share its goodness with others. In Jesus' name, amen.**

Before dismissing your children hold up your open grab bag. **Next time you come to church, bring a can of food with you. Let's see if we can stuff my grab bag with food for our church pantry. This way when families in our community need a good breakfast—or dinner—they can stop by and pick up what they need—bear nips and all!**

Home Sweet Home

On Your Mark

Bible Truth: We are loved and highly valued by God.

Bible Verse: The LORD is the one who keeps you safe. So let the Most High God be like a home to you (Psalm 91:9).

Godprint: Preciousness

Get Set

Grab Bag: Bible, hamster cage or other small animal cage (if you have a small animal, bring that along too!), animal crackers

GO!

A nice lady in a pet store once told me that it's pets that make a house a home. In other words, pets make a house a special place to be. What do you think?

• What pet would you like to have?
• What really, really *big* pet would you like to have?

When I go to the zoo with my (daughter, son, niece, nephew), **he/she tells me to open the trunk of the car because she wants to take home all of the animals. And not just the cute little baby rabbits or chicks at the petting zoo! No, she wants the rhino, the full-grown llamas and the whole herd of spotted giraffes!** Reach into your grab bag and pass out the animal crackers.

• Would these animals feel at home in your house?

Once we get home I explain that this (pull out the hamster cage from your grab bag) **is about the size of it! Whatever fits in this cage is a pet we can have. This is all our small house can hold. I love tigers and bears and all the tiny deer that live in the rain forest, but their home is not here with us.**

For the creatures of the world, the earth is their home. Have children stomp the "earth" with their feet. **God created prairies and hillsides, mountains and thickets, deserts and wetlands for all the big and small animals he cares about.**

And the earth is our home too. But God tells us that because we are precious to him, our home is also in him. Listen to our Scripture verse from the Book of Psalms. Read Psalm 91:9.

• What does this verse tell us God does for us?
• How is God like a home to us?

Hmm. Wherever we are we're already home—in God's care! In his arms we receive many, "I'm-so-glad-you're-here-with-me!" hugs. Ask children to wrap themselves up in a big hug.

• Do you think God likes hugs and kisses?

When we're wet and tired, God is home—with words of comfort.

• How is God's Word in the Bible like a warm blanket on a chilly day?

And when we feel bad and sad inside, God is home—with words of kindness and a smile of forgiveness.

Let's pray and rejoice with God who thinks we're lovable and hugable. Pause for prayer. **Dear God, in you we're loved and honored. Because your love light shines so bright, we know you're always home.** Dismiss your children with hugs. **Welcome home!**

In a Nutshell

On Your Mark

Bible Truth: God gives us strength when we need it most.

Bible Verse: But [the Lord] said to me, "My grace is all you need, my power is strongest when you are weak." So I am very happy to brag about how weak I am. Then Christ's power can rest on me (2 Corinthians 12:9).

Godprint: Perseverance

Get Set

Grab Bag: Bible, walnuts in the shells, an old college textbook or dictionary, a bowl

Ahead of time, set your grab bag out of sight of your children.

GO!

Welcome your children with a warm smile. **Oops! I forgot something.** Excuse yourself to get your grab bag. With exaggerated effort, drag it towards your chair. Ask two or three of your children if they wouldn't mind giving you a hand and lifting the grab bag to your lap. Thank your helpers and then take out the bag of walnuts.

My strength's not what it used to be! But thank God his is. Hand out the walnuts, one per child. **Now let's see how strong** *you* **are. Use your hands and crack your walnut. No teeth!** Obviously this will be difficult.

Hard? But hey, that's okay. God doesn't mind whether or not you can crack walnuts or lift heavy bags or jump buildings in a single bound. In fact, God tells us that when we're weak, we're strong. Pause. **Let me say that again. In God's eyes, when we're** *weak***, we're strong!**

Scratch your head. **Hmm. Just like our nuts, this may be hard for us to crack. But here goes! When we're weak we need God…we need his grace and strength. We need to rely on him. So when we're weak, God can shine through us and show the world what** *he's* **made of.** Open you Bible and read 2 Corinthians 12:9.

• According to this verse, what is all we need? *(God's grace; God's power.)*
• What do you think happens when Christ's power rests on us?

Wow. We hear the Apostle Paul happy, even bragging, about his weaknesses. Hmm. There must be something to this! With God's wisdom and strength all things are possible.

Reach inside your grab bag and remove the old college textbook. Open the book and lay it on the floor in front of you. Have children place their walnuts, two at a time, on one of the pages. Gently close the book on the walnuts and have children use both hands to push down on the cover. The nuts will crack easily! Collect the nutmeats and shells in a bowl after each round. After service you can gather the nuts from the bowl and whip up a loaf of banana bread to share at your next Bible study.

You had strength you didn't know you had! That's the way it is with God. His power helps us do things we never thought we could do on our own. God gives us his strength when we need it most. Let's pray and allow God's power to work in us.

Bow heads to pray. **Dear God, you are great and powerful. Let your mighty strength work in us for your good. In Jesus' name, amen.**

LifeGod

On Your Mark

Bible Truth: We're glad that God is with us and cares for us.

Bible Verse: God, your thoughts about me are priceless. No one can possibly add them all up. If I could count them, they would be more than the grains of sand. If I were to fall asleep counting and then wake up, you would still be there with me (Psalm 139:17-18).

Godprint: Joy

Get Set

Grab Bag: Bible, a beach hat and sunglasses, a 1-gallon freezer zip-top bag with sand in the bottom, shaving gel, wet wipes for sticky fingers. Optional: marbles

GO!

Put on your beach hat and sunglasses. **Back from the beach! I had a great time. Did you?** Pause. **Yes, the day was warm and bright and the water was perfect. We made sand castles, put on gobs of sun lotion and ate sand-crunchy bologna sandwiches.** Yawn and stretch. **I'm tuckered out. A nap sounds good just about now!**

• Who watches over you when you take a nap?
• Have you ever fallen asleep in the car? Who gets you home safe while you sleep?

Take off your sunglasses. Then reach into your grab bag and take out the zip-top bag. **I collected some of the sand from the beach before we left as a reminder of our wonderful day together. Today's Scripture tells us that God remembers our days too.** Remove your beach hat and plop the zip-top bag of sand on your head. **Let's see. Scripture tells us that God's mind is like a sandbag!** Pause. **No, that's not it.** Pause again. **I've got it! We make God's mind sandy!** Pause and frown. **No, that's not it either.** Remove the bag from your head. **What I mean to say is that we are on God's mind all the time. In fact, if we could count all his thoughts about us they would outnumber all the grains of sand in this bag. It's true!** Open your Bible to Psalm 139:17, 18. Hand it to a volunteer to read aloud.

• What's the highest number you can count to?
• How many grains of sand do you think there are on a beach?

• How many times a day do you think God thinks about you?

God knows all about you and you and you! Point to your children. **God thinks of you when you're playing on the beach, collecting shells and even when you're napping. Wherever we are, God knows what's up.** Reach into your grab bag and pull out the shaving gel can.

I need five volunteer squirts!

Hand the shaving gel can to a child and have him or her squirt some inside the zip-top bag. **God knows where you go.** Pass the can to another child to squirt.

God knows who you are. Another squirt!

God knows what you think. Another squirt!

God knows what you love. Another squirt!

And…God knows what's in your heart.

Like a jellyfish, it's see-through! If you brought marbles, have an older volunteer take them from your grab bag. Have children drop a few "hearts" into the sandbag. (Marbles are choking hazards for young children, so supervise carefully.)

Press out the extra air from the zip-top sandbag and then zip it closed. Lay the bag in front of you and ask children to press on it. Foamy waves will suddenly appear and your children will see their sandy, water-clear hearts rise and fall. **Surf's up!**

Make room in your beach bag for the Heavenly Father who knows you best. Don't forget that God's your LifeGod. Yawn a final time. **Unlike us, his watchful eyes are always on duty. Let's pray and thank God for always being with us.**

Bow heads to pray. **Heavenly Father, thank you for thinking about us and watching over us. We're glad that you're with us even when we're asleep. In Jesus' name, amen.**

Oodles of Noodles

On Your Mark

Bible Truth: God wants us to use our skills and knowledge to honor him.

Bible Verse: The LORD gives wisdom. Knowledge and understanding come from his mouth...You will understand what is right and honest and fair. You will understand the right way to live. Your heart will become wise. Your mind will delight in knowledge (Proverbs 2:6–10).

Godprint: Wisdom

Get Set

Grab Bag: Bible, cup of dry noodle soup, drinking glass, a nickel, index card. Optional: bottled water

GO!

Reach into your grab bag and pull out the cup of noodle soup. Give the cup a shake. **An old saying tells us that the way to solve problems is to *use your noodle*. No, not the kind in here** (shake the cup of soup) **but the kind in here** (point to your head). **When we use our brainpower we're *using our noodles* to figure things out.**

• Did you use your noodle this week in school or at home? *(That's a no-brainer! We noodle every day at school.)*
• When Mom or Dad are too busy to help, how do you solve problems on your own?

Let's try to noodle a tough problem right now. The congregation can help too. Set the cup of soup aside and take the drinking glass, nickel and index card from your grab bag. Hold the drinking glass in your hand. Ask an older volunteer to place the index card on top of the glass and the nickel in the middle of the card. **Our problem to noodle is this: How can we get this nickel to drop inside the cup without a) touching the nickel, b) lifting the card or c) touching the card with our fingertips.** Have children noodle over this for a minute or two. If necessary, explain why suggestions they make won't work: **I'm sorry, but that won't work, Jeremy. That's lifting the card.** Go ahead and ask the congregation for their "two-cents."

After a while say, **Wow. We have oodles of noodles working on this one!**

Put the drinking cup aside for now. **When we use our noodles—our brains—and make the wise choice to read the Bible, God gives us the wisdom to figure out tough things like who he is, what makes him smile and laugh and the difference between right and wrong.** Hold up your Bible. It's all in here! **When we search God's Word we find the truth and learn how to use our noodles to honor him. As our Bible verse for today says, all wisdom comes from God.** Open your Bible and ask a reader to read Proverbs 2:6–10.

• According to these verses, what does God give us? *(Wisdom, knowledge, understanding.)*
• Why is it important for us to have these things?

Are we ready to try this again? Pick up the drinking cup with the index card and nickel and hold it away from your children. Then, using your thumb and pointer finger, "snap" or "flick" the edge of the card. Your fingernail does all the work! The card will shoot away from the cup and the nickel will drop neatly inside. **Use your noodle in ways that honor God!** Allow one or two children to give the trick a try before putting all items away.

Bow heads for prayer. **Dear God, thank you for giving us wisdom. When we have to figure out problems, help us to make wise choices that honor you. In your name we pray, amen.**

If you brought a water bottle, uncap it now. Remove the lid from the cup of soup you put aside earlier and pour in the water. **If you'd like, join me after service. We'll have one or two brave volunteers close their eyes and place their hands into the cup of soup—to feel their oodles of noodles hard at work!**

Sunshine in a Jar

On Your Mark

Bible Truth: God responds to us in love.

Bible Verse: His great love is new every morning. LORD, how faithful you are! (Lamentations 3:23).

Godprint: Love

Get Set

Grab Bag: Bible, a container of TicTac® mint candies, a small, empty and narrow jar with cover (a small spice jar works well), sharpened pencil, a bag of Pixy Stix® candy

Ahead of time, tear open three or four of the same-color candy sticks and pour the powder inside the jar. Cover the jar and set it inside your grab bag.

GO!

Good morning! Take the mint candies from your grab bag and pop one into your mouth. Then distribute the candy to all outstretched hands. **Long ago there was a popular song on the radio about a man who made delicious candy. His name was the Candy Man. Everything the Candy Man did made the world taste good! Even when skies were gray and smiles were frowns, the Candy Man could whip up a delicious candy surprise and the world was a better place.**

• What is your favorite candy?
• Why does a sweet treat bring sunny smiles together?

Lick your lips. **All gone! I think sweet candy and good times are a lot alike. Even with the best Candy Man in town, it's just a matter of time before we run out of the sweet stuff.**

• If a candy could fill you with love, what flavor would it be?
• What would it be like if you could try a new flavor of candy every morning?

Open your Bible and read Lamentations 3:23.

• What does this verse say about God's love?

Good news, everyone! Don't fret! Don't worry! Don't lose heart! God promises us that his sunny sweet love is new every morning. Each day his love burns bright for you and me. Remove the partially filled jar you prepared ahead of time from your grab bag. Distribute the Pixy Stix candies. Let's make our own sunny day—and keep it in a jar to remember God's great love. Through good and bad, sweet and sad times, we can delight in God's promise of a bright tomorrow.

Hold out the jar. Look. I grabbed a few rays of sunshine on my way to church this morning! Let's add more. Have children carefully tear the tops off their candy sticks and take turns pouring the colored sugar into the jar.

• If you had love enough to fill a candy store, who would you share it with?

Grab hold of the pencil from your bag and hand it off to a shy child in your group. Ask him or her to stick the pencil down in the jar and poke along the sides to stir the powder gently. This will create delicate designs.

When the children are done pouring, nod to a child near you. Quick! Cover the jar before our sunshine escapes! If the jar is not full, tell your children that you will finish filling the jar with colored sugar and display it where everyone can see it. Each day is a new beginning in the love of God.

Gather children to pray. Dear God, may we never lose the miracle of your bright love. In Jesus' name, amen.

Sweet Dreams

On Your Mark

Bible Truth: God is in control; we can depend on him.

Bible Story: Joseph dreams and is sold into slavery (Genesis 37:1–36).

Godprint: Hope

Get Set

Grab Bag: Bible, dried wheat stalks (or similar item), star stickers

GO!

Welcome and thank you for joining me. Today I'd like you to close your eyes and take a nice deep breath. Go ahead! Pause while children settle down. **Now think of the best dream you've ever had. I'll just sit here and wait while you dream away.**

Whistle a happy hymn as you wait. After a while wake up your children! A few will be bursting to share their wonderful dreams. **My, my. And in color too?** Open your Bible to Genesis 37. **From the pages of the Bible comes a boy named Joseph. He was a dreamer too. He lived with his 11 brothers in a land called Canaan a long time ago. One night Joseph had a spectacular dream.**

Read Genesis 37:5–7. Hold up the wheat stalks. **All the field's grain bowed to Joseph's grain!** Ask children to stand and stretch. **Now pretend you are stalks of wheat and show me a deep bow.** Pause as children bow. **Yes, just like that.** Have children remain standing. **Well, Joseph had another dream. And this one was "star-tacular!"**

Read Genesis 37:9, 10. Pass out the star stickers. **This time Joseph saw stars—and the moon and the sun. The stars bowed down to him as well.** Ask children to throw their star stickers up into the air. **Now "bow" over and pick them up.** Have children gather stickers and sit down.

• How would it feel to have the stars bow to you?

Now Joseph's brothers weren't about to bow down to their younger brother. No way! So the jealous brothers sold Joseph to men traveling with camels. Joseph *could* **have been angry.** Shake your fist in the air. Have the children do the same. **He** *could* **have shouted,**

"No way! I'm not riding on a stinky camel!" Have children repeat the phrase after you.

Joseph was sad to travel so far away from home, but he trusted God to see him through. He did his very best and kept trusting God. He didn't stop believing that God was in control. And God blessed him. Joseph ended up in Egypt, where he became an important leader to help the country through hard times.

The next time a stinky camel thing happens to you and you're not sure who's in control, raise your voice! Shout with your children. Ask the congregation to join you. God is in control. Pause. I can trust him. Pause. Even when a stinky camel comes to call!

Bow heads to pray. Mighty God, we know that whatever happens to us, you are in control. Help us to keep on trusting you and keep on doing what you want us to do. Amen.

Wisdom Tooth Truth

On Your Mark

Bible Truth: We can use the skills and knowledge God gives us to honor him.

Bible Verse: For the LORD gives wisdom, and from his mouth come knowledge and understanding (Proverbs 2:6).

Godprint: Wisdom

Get Set

Grab Bag: Bible, toothbrush, an empty, clean coffee or juice drink bottle 3/4 full with dry rice, Scrabble® letters or Boggle® cubes in a bag

GO!

Grab the toothbrush from your bag. **When I was your age I kept my teeth in a jar by my bed.** Pause. **Oops! What I mean to say is when I was little I'd keep the teeth that fell out in a jar by my bed. The next morning I'd often awake to find a $1 bill tucked under the jar and the tooth gone. Wow! It seemed a wise choice, teeth for cash!**

• Do we have any loose teeth in the crowd today?

When you're a little older, you might get "wisdom teeth." But you'll soon learn they don't really make you wise. God tells us that wisdom does not come from "wisdom teeth" or jars filled with money. Wisdom comes from him. If we want to understand and learn about him, we need to read his Word.

Open your Bible and read Proverbs 2:6 or have a volunteer read the verse.

Everything you ever wanted to know, God knows. Compared to God we have the wisdom of a toad!

• If God hired you to write a book of "The Hardest Questions Ever!" which one would you want answered first?
• How does God want you to use your wisdom and experience to help a younger brother or sister?

Take the jar filled with rice from your grab bag as well as the Scrabble letters. Remove the jar's lid and trace your finger around the mouth of the jar. **This part of the jar is known as the "mouth?" It is! Let's take turns picking letters from the letter bag and naming things that describe our wise God that begin with that letter. Once you've made a match drop your letter into the mouth of the bottle.** Word examples might include: Almighty, Awesome, Creator, Caring, Deliverer, Divine, Eternal, Everlasting, Faithful, Father, Forgiving, Friend, Generous, Great, Head, Healer, Helpful, Holy, King, I Am, Life, Love, Loyal, Merciful, Ruler, Spirit, Truth, Wise, Worthy, Wonderful, Yahweh.

After children have dropped in letters, place the lid on the jar. Give it a good shake. The letters will settle in and around the rice.

Our mouth is filled with wisdom! Hand the bottle to a child. **Now give it a good shake. When a letter appears, think hard and see if you can remember what the letter stood for. If not, simply shout out a new word. God won't mind a bit!** Allow children to take turns shaking and shouting. After a while gather your children A.S.A.P for Always Say A Prayer time.

What's your name for God? Whatever you choose, use it often. Let's pray. Pause. Thank you, Wise, Generous, Almighty and Merciful God, for helping us to see that the truth is right where it ought to be—in your Word, the Bible. Amen.

I Yam

On Your Mark

Bible Truth: Because Jesus loves me I can put my faith in him.
Bible Story: Jesus says, "I am" (John 6:35; 8:12; 10:7; 11:25; 14:6; 15:5).
Godprint: Faith

Get Set

Grab Bag: a Bible with sticky notes marking the "I am" passages, pictures cut from the reproducible sheet (p. 32), blank nametags and a pen

Ahead of time, push a "standing" yam into the exposed part of a nail that has been driven through a block of wood. Push six pushpins into your yam "bulletin board."

GO!

Make nametags for a few of your early "sitters."

Nametags are wonderful helpers for pastors. Thank you for wearing yours. Hold up your Bible and open it to the Old Testament. Lay it on the floor in front of you. **In the Old Testament if God had a printed nametag it would read like this.** Pick up your pen and write "I AM" on an extra nametag. Hold it up for kids to read. **That's right. God's nametag would read, "I AM." These two little words told God's people that he was the real deal...the all knowing, almighty, trustworthy, one-and-only God, worthy of all the best.**

Flip your Bible to the New Testament. **In the New Testament God's only Son, Jesus, also uses the words "I AM" to describe himself. But this time he ties them to other words to help people understand who he is.** Ask for six volunteer readers. Hand your Bible to reader #1.

Jesus certainly doesn't need a billboard to tell the world who he is. But a yam might be helpful! Carefully remove the yam "bulletin board" from your grab bag and set it in front of you. **I'll start each sentence with the words "I am." My wonderful readers will finish it using the Bible.** Reach into your grab bag and take out the six pictures cut from the reproducible. **After each verse I'll need a volunteer to pin a picture to our bulletin board so we don't forget all the "I am" things Jesus said about himself. Let's get started. Reader #1, you're up!**

John 6:35:   I am…the bread of life. *Pause.* Have a child pin the picture of the loaf of bread to the yam bulletin board.

John 8:12:   I am…the light of the world. *Pause.* Pin the picture of the light bulb to the yam bulletin board.

John 10:7:   I am…the gate for the sheep. *Pause.* Pin the picture of the sheep pen.

John 11:25:   I am…the resurrection and the life. *Pause.* Pin the picture of the resurrected Jesus.

John 14:6:   I am…the way and the truth and the life. *Pause.* Pin the picture of the meadow path.

John 15:5:   I am…the vine. *Pause.* Finally, pin the picture of the grapes on a vine.

Our yam bulletin board is pretty stuffed. And that's good!

• Why do you think Jesus used these "word pictures" to help people understand what he was saying about himself?

• Which one is your favorite?

This will be a great reminder for us to always put our faith in Jesus. Pause to pray. **Dear God, thank you for sending your Son, Jesus. Let our love and faith increase in him. Amen.**

Hold up the yam bulletin board for one final look. **Thanks for spending time with me today. "I yam" very glad you did!**

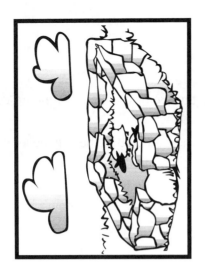

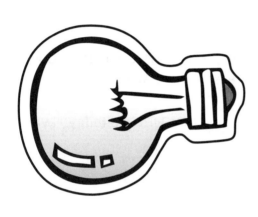

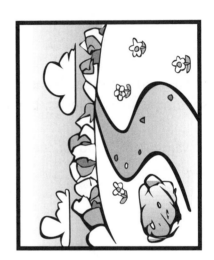

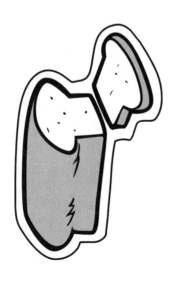

I Love God!

Our loving God created us to be in a relationship with him. Each new day brings new opportunities for us to show God we love him, to honor him, to use our abilities to serve him, to turn away from our bad choices and to follow him wholeheartedly. When we believe in Jesus, God makes us new. Now we live as God's children, ready to share our joy in him with other people. We're confident because we know God is in control. We can trust Jesus at all times. When we stray from God's way, we can always come back to his arms open in love. Worship. Prayer. Faith. Trust. We show our love to God in all these ways.

A Coat of Oil

On Your Mark

Bible Truth: God is great. We have deep respect for his power.

Bible Verse: Nothing is impossible with God (Luke 1:37).

Godprint: Reverence

Get Set

Grab Bag: Bible, bag of 8-inch balloons, jar of cooking oil, wooden skewer

You may want to practice the balloon-skewer instructions before you give your sermon.

GO!

I love to hear so many different sounds. The sound of a meadowlark in a field of summer flowers, the clink of hot chocolate mugs on a winter afternoon and the choir singing a special hymn anytime of year. Close your eyes and listen for your special sound.

• What sounds put a smile on your face?
• What sound makes you feel happy and safe inside?

Open your eyes. Now let's switch gears a little. **Name a sound that makes you jump or one that frightens you.** As children share their thoughts, reach into your grab bag and pull out the bag of balloons. Take a balloon and stretch it. Blow it three-fourths full, then knot it closed. Reach into your grab bag again and take out the wooden skewer. With as much drama as possible, bring the sharp end of the skewer perilously close to the balloon.

Anyone care to take a guess what sound I do *not* like to hear? Listen to the squeals and shrieks of dreaded anticipation. **Yes, it's the popping of a balloon!**

But what if I were to say that I could poke this wooden stick into the balloon without popping it? *Impossible!* Put down the balloon and the skewer and pick up your Bible. Ask a volunteer to read Luke 1:37.

Nothing is impossible with God. Isn't that wonderful? He made the air inside my balloon.

In fact, he made all of nature. Do you like looking up at the stars? Even with today's modern telescopes, scientists cannot count all the stars in the night sky. God is great, and he can do things that human beings can only dream of doing.

• Name some other wonderful things God has done that would be impossible for humans to do.

God is good. When you feel afraid or when the world seems a mean, hurtful place, remember the greatness of God. He wants to use his great power to help you. Nothing is impossible with his loving kindness.

Put your Bible down and pick up the balloon and skewer again. **I say that it is possible to stick this balloon and not have it pop. Shall we give it a try?** Many of your children will rush to cover their ears.

Reach in your bag and grab the jar of oil. Dip the skewer into the oil. Coat it well. Then look for the dark rubber "circle" at the top of your balloon. This is the thick part of the balloon skin. With a slow, twisting action, twist the skewer into this spot. Go ahead and twist! Keep twisting until the point of the skewer breaks through the balloon skin—with nary a sound or whoosh of air! If you're feeling bold, keep twisting until the skewer breaks through the bottom (the tied end) of the balloon. You may wish to give this a try a few times before church to get the hang—or bang!—of it.

Pop! If your balloon happens to pop during your children's talk, simply say to your captive audience, **Nothing is impossible with God, but anything is possible in a children's sermon!** Then try it again. Allow children to take a close look at the balloon with the skewer in it. **Some of you didn't think this was possible. Once in a while we all feel like something is impossible. But God is great and he can do anything. This balloon with the skewer through it reminds us of that!**

Gather children to pray. **Thank you, God, for your greatness and awesome power. Nothing is impossible with you. Amen!**

A Psalmwich to Go

On Your Mark

Bible Truth: God wants us to honor him for his greatness.

Bible Story: Psalm 67

Godprint: Praise

Get Set

Grab Bag: Bible, Lunchables® pack, plate, box of sandwich crackers

You can find Lunchables® in the lunchmeat section of the grocery store.

GO!

Kids will recognize and enjoy the fun, stackable ingredients in a Lunchables® kit. If you can't pick up one, use lunchmeat, sliced cheese and two pieces of bread. Or if the size of your group permits, cut circles from lunchmeat and sliced cheese, and have kids build individual psalmwiches on circle crackers as you give the sermon.

Once children settle down, greet them with a sneeze! Listen for one or two "God bless yous" from your children and perhaps from the congregation. Return the kindness with an **And may God bless you!** of your own.

• Besides sneezing times, what other times do we need God's blessings?

That's right. All the time! We want God's blessings all the time so we can live happily in his grace. When God blesses us, we want to praise him. Any time is blessing time. Even lunchtime! Let's read Psalm 67 and build a tasty "psalmwich" filled with praises for our Lord God.

Reach into your grab bag and take out the plate and Lunchables® kit. Hand your Bible to a reader. Read Psalm 67:1, 2. Place the plate on your lap. Take a cracker from the Lunchables® pack and set it on the plate.

• What family blessing do you say at home before mealtimes?

I feel mighty blessed that you are all here today. It's important that I share God's saving Word with your hungry hearts. Ask another reader to continue the Psalm and read verse 3.

Take a piece of meat and a piece of cheese and stack them on your cracker.

• We have a lot of people in church today. What a blessing it would be if we were to invite the whole church to lunch! What would we serve?
• How could we praise God together while we had lunch?

God wants the whole world to praise him for his blessings. We need to share not only our lunch, but also God's Word with others so they can come to know him as we do. Ask another reader to continue the Psalm reading with verse 4.

Stack more cheese and meat circles on your cracker.

• How does singing songs of praise make you joyful?
• Which one is your favorite?

Remember what we said at the beginning of our talk? God's blessings make people happy. To be ruled by a just and fair God makes me happy. How about you? Ask another reader to continue the Psalm reading with verses 5 and 6.

God blesses us with food. He sends the rain and sun that the crops need to grow. That's another blessing we can praise God for.

Finish up the Psalm and your "psalmwich" with verse 7.

Top off your stack of meat and cheese with another cracker. Look at your plate. Lunch is served! Hmm. This "psalmwich" looks yummy, but I think I'll save it for lunch.

Put the plate aside and take the sandwich crackers from your grab bag. Shake the box. Sounds good. Let's say grace before we munch. Pause to pray. Dear God, we praise your greatness and thank you for this food. In Jesus' name, amen. Open the box and offer crackers to your children.

Why not pick a joyful praise psalm and build a "psalmwich" of your own for lunch today?

Optional: Let children serve sandwich crackers to others in the congregation as they go back to their seats.

Whale of a Good Time

On Your Mark

Bible Truth: God wants us to follow his instructions.

Bible Verse: But the LORD sent a huge fish to swallow Jonah. And Jonah was inside the fish for three days and three nights (Jonah 1:17).

Godprint: Obedience

Get Set

Grab Bag: Bible, foam cups, marker

GO!

Follow the leader! I have a follow-the-leader activity for us to play today. You'll have to obey me and follow my instructions so that we can do the motions together and at the same time. Make sure to practice the hand jive below ahead of time so you can perform it for your children. Or simplify it using your own movements.

Clap knees. (2x)
Clap hands. (2x)
Tap your right fist under your left elbow. (2x)
Tap your left fist under your right elbow. (2x)
Tap your right fist on top of your left fist. (2x)
Tap your left fist on top of your right fist. (2x)
Pass your right hand, palm down, over the top of your left hand. (2x)
Pass your left hand, palm down, over the top of your right hand. (2x)
Point your right thumb over your right shoulder. (2x)
Point your left thumb over your left shoulder. (2x)

Practice the motions with your children. Start very slowly then quicken the pace. Don't be surprised if children get all mixed up. **Sarah, you missed the elbow tap. Jonathan, you forgot to clap twice!** Turn to the congregation. **Will you give us a hand?** Try the motions again with the entire church body. Speed up the motions to get everyone moving. After a while offer a round of applause for a very fine effort by all.

• What would happen if someone decided to make up their own motions instead of following my instructions?

Today's Bible verse talks about a man who did not obey instructions very well. He didn't even want to try because he didn't like the instructions God gave him. Who can tell me a little about the Bible story of Jonah and the very large fish? (Some of the children will know something about the Jonah Bible story. God told Jonah to go to Nineveh to preach to the people. Jonah disobeyed and ran away to the sea. A storm came, and Jonah knew it was his fault. The sailors threw him off the ship and a large fish swallowed him. Jonah prayed for God to save him. God did and this time Jonah obeyed God and preached in Nineveh that the people should stop living lives of evil.)

Good job! Let's find out what Jonah was thinking about when he was inside that big fish. Ask a reader to read Jonah 2:7–10.

• How did Jonah's attitude change inside the fish?
• Why does God want us to obey him even when we think it's the wrong thing to do?

Hand each child a foam cup from your grab bag. Also take out the marker. **Let's make fish cup puppets to remind us of the big fish in the Jonah story and how we should obey God and not run away when he calls.** Show children how to press a finger into the bottoms of their cups until the bottoms split. Press in the sides to form a lovely pair of fish lips! Use a marker to draw on eyes. Then watch as small hands fit inside the cups to squeeze the fish lips open and closed.

• What will this fish cup help you remember?

God cares about all people—even the ones who turn fish tail and run! Again and again God brings us back to him. Thank you, God! Gather children for prayer. **Dear God, help us to obey you even when we don't want to. Help us to obey our parents too. In Jesus' name, amen.** Have children take their fish cups back to their seats.

Cup Your Hands

On Your Mark

Bible Truth: God wants us to turn away from our bad choices and follow him.

Bible Verse: But your sins were washed away. You were made holy. You were made right with God. All of that was done in the name of the Lord Jesus Christ and by the Spirit of our God (1 Corinthians 6:11).

Godprint: Repentance

Get Set

Grab Bag: Bible, computer keyboard, two 9-ounce clear plastic cups, permanent marker, stickers in the shape of children or happy face stickers

Before church, adhere the stickers to the outside of one of the plastic cups. Drop this cup inside the other so that the stickers show through and the outer cup twists freely.

GO!

As children gather, take the computer keyboard out of your grab bag and place it on your lap. **Type intently. Oh, hello. I'm sorry. I didn't hear you sit down. I'm working very hard on a short story—which I'd like your help with today. I'm stuck on one important word. Please raise your hand if you can help me.** Begin your story.

"One cold and stormy night little red circles suddenly popped up on my computer screen. Error! Error! they screamed. With a final gasp my computer screen turned blue and died. Alas. I knew all was lost because I'd forgotten to ___ my work. The *Very Sad* End!"

Applaud the child who raises his or her hand and shouts, "SAVE!"

You've got it! Return your computer keyboard to the grab bag and take out the cups you prepared ahead of time and the marker. **God sent his only Son, Jesus, to save us, not from awful computer crashes, but from our sins that shout, "Me first!" and "My way always!"** Hold the cups high so children can see the bright children stickers. **Let's think. What wrongs keep us from being close to God? Angry words? Selfish hands? When you think of something, come up and use this marker to place an "x" on the cup. As you make your mark, share your thought with the group.**

After a while many unsightly "xs" will cover the outside of the cup. Twist the outer cup for kids to see how the marks affect them all. Then put the cups aside for a moment and open your Bible. Read 1 Corinthians 6:11 or ask a volunteer to do it.

• What does this verse say happens to our sins? *(They are washed away.)*
• How can our sins be forgiven? *(By God's power. In Jesus' name.)*

God wants us to ask forgiveness for the wrongs we do. Let's bring that very thought to him in prayer now.

Have children bow their heads in prayer. **Dear God, please forgive our sins and help us do things the way Jesus would. In his name, amen.**

Pick up the cups again. **With Christ's forgiveness we are clean and spotless again.** Ask a volunteer to lift the inner cup from the outer one. The "children" appear new and unmarked. **We're brand new in Christ!**

Before children head back to their seats say, **When you get home, "cup your hands" and make your own saving cup. Think of the wrongs that you just prayed about. Take two cups and place one inside the other like we just did. Then dip the bottom of the cups into dirty dishwater! Before the water reaches too high remove the inner cup. See how Jesus washes away our sins with bubbles of forgiveness!**

Four Karats

On Your Mark

Bible Truth: When we believe in Jesus, God makes us new.

Bible Verse: Anyone who believes in Christ is a new creation. The old is gone! The new has come! (2 Corinthians 5:17).

Godprint: Faith

Get Set

Grab Bag: Bible, a white paper tablecloth, fresh carrots cut in two, red inkpad, green markers. Optional: little note cards (blank 3x5 index cards folded over would do nicely)

GO!

Spread out the tablecloth on the floor. **Come join me today and help me get ready for a picnic lunch!** Have children gather and sit around the skirt of the tablecloth. Pull out the cut carrots from your bag and drop them in the middle of the tablecloth. **Yum! What's a picnic without ripe, juicy cherries?** Wait for a response from your children. Their reactions might sound something like this: *Those are carrots. My mom chops them up and puts them in the salad for dinner. Cherries are red. My bunny likes to eat those.*

Hmm. You say carrot, I say cherry. How can one thing be something else? In today's Scripture the Apostle Paul tells us that if we believe in Jesus we are something else—new creations in him. Hand the Bible to a reader in your group. Ask him or her to read 2 Corinthians 5:17.

- Do you like the feel of new clothes at Christmas or Easter?
- What do you think it means to be a new creation?
- What would make you feel brand new on the inside?

Reach in your bag and pull out the inkpads. Lay them opened near the carrots. Then have children take turns picking up the carrots and pressing the cut ends into the inkpad, and onto the tablecloth. Red cherry circles should appear. **A new creation!** Reach in your bag and pull out the green markers. **I think our carrot-cherries could use stems and a few green leaves.** Have children work side by side stamping cherry circles and making stems and leaves to go with them. Pretty soon you'll have a wonderful tablecloth for the next church picnic!

When we have faith in Christ and stay committed to him we want to become like him. Outside we may look the same. But inside we're faith-filled. And with faith comes Jesus' joy, Jesus' patience, Jesus' love, Jesus' grace, and Jesus' hope for a life forever with him. Close the inkpads and collect the carrots and markers.

Let's pray to our God who gives us all things. Pause for prayer. **Dear God, make me a new creation in Christ, amen.**

If time allows, distribute the note cards. Before dismissing your children, press a cherry circle on each card. **When you get home, finish decorating the little note card I just stamped. Ask Mom or Dad to help you write, "I am a new creation in Jesus!" anywhere inside the card.**

Freckled Smiles

On Your Mark

Bible Truth: God wants us to show our joy in him to other people.

Bible Verse: A happy heart makes a face look cheerful. But a sad heart produces a broken spirit (Proverbs 15:13).

Godprint: Joy

Get Set

Grab Bag: Bible, two permanent markers, balloons, a lap tray, paper circle confetti

GO!

Raise your hand if you've ever had the chicken pox. Pause. **Two?** (Or whatever number matches the hands raised.) **Is that all?** Look out to the moms and dads in the congregation. **How about the moms and dads out there?** Pause and count up. **Poor things! Chicken pox was and is a very contagious disease. You might have had a shot so that you wouldn't get chicken pox. But when I was young, chicken pox was always looking for someone to play catch!**

But there is something else that is super contagious that I hope I catch every day. Anyone care to take a guess? Listen to your children's responses.

Close! I'm talking about smiles.

Ask children to turn and face the congregation. **On the count of three, show everyone out there your very best smile. One...two...three!** Watch as the congregation suddenly catches smile-itis! **Look at all the happy faces! The congregation has caught your smiles. No doubt about it, smiles are contagious.**

Opposite time! Now show me your saddest frown—one that says, "I'm just too pooped to bother with a smile today." Take a look at all the frowns. **I think I just caught your frown.** Turn to the congregation. **Oops! So did they! Hmm. Oh, no, this just won't do.**

Draw your children's attention back to you. Place your pointer fingers on the corners of your mouth and nudge a smile back to your face. Have your children and the congregation do the same. **Much,**

much better. Let's give our congregation a round of applause for catching all we had to give! Pause as children clap with cheerful smiles and hands.

Open your Bible to Proverbs 15:13 and read the verse aloud.

• What does this verse say about a happy heart?
• How does your face show what's in your heart?

It seems that both smiles *and* frowns are contagious. Which one would you rather catch? A cheerful smile gets my vote too!

Reach into your grab bag and pull out the balloons. Distribute them to your group. Ask volunteers from the congregation to help inflate balloons and tie knots for the younger children. As volunteers work, pull the tray and paper confetti from your grab bag. Set the tray on your lap and sprinkle on a little confetti. If time is a concern, you may prefer to inflate the balloons in advance and keep them all in a large garbage bag.

Look around to make sure every child has a balloon. **I see we're ready to make faces! Remember smiling faces will help others see Jesus.** Take the marker from the bag and draw a smiley face on each child's balloon. Have your helpers lend a hand too.

May I use your head, please? Rub your balloon on a child's hair and bring the balloon close to the paper circles on the tray. Watch as the circles dance a bit before jumping onto the balloon. **Freckles! Now these spots I love to see on happy children's faces. That looks really cheerful. Your balloon will remind you that a happy heart makes a face look cheerful.**

Bow heads in prayer. **Dear God, thank you for giving us faces. Help us to show on our faces that we have happy hearts because we know you and love you. In Jesus' name, amen.**

Have children give their "faces" a rub to pick up a few freckles before heading back to their seats.

Give It a Squirt

Bible Truth: God is in control, so I can be confident.

Bible Story: Gideon and 300 men defeat the Midianites (Judges 6:15; 7:1–8, 16–21).

Godprint: Confidence

Get Set

Grab Bag: Bible, picnic blanket and basket, package of hot dog buns

GO!

Spread out the picnic blanket and ask children to have a seat. Place the picnic basket by your side. **Greetings! Happy Picnic Day. Just imagine that I'm firing up the barbecue grill. In no time at all I'm cooking juicy hamburgers and tasty hot dogs.** Take a whiff. **Doesn't that smell good?**

Reach in the picnic basket and take out the hot dog buns. Tear the buns apart and hand them to your children. **What toppings do you like on your hot dog?** Pause. **Mmm. I like that too!** Take a look in your picnic basket. **Oh, no! I've forgotten the mustard and catsup, pickles, cheese, chili, onions...** (add your children's' favorite toppings). Scratch your head. **You know, a squirt of mustard isn't a very big thing. But it certainly is the difference between a plain old hot dog and one that's delicious.**

- If you could be a hot dog topping which one would you choose?
- How can a little topping pack a mighty punch to a picnic lunch?

Gideon, the Bible character in today's story, was a squirt! In other words, he wasn't very big on the confidence menu. The Bible also tells us he was the youngest in his family (Judges 6:15). I think Gideon probably felt pretty weak and puny—certainly not mighty enough to lead 300 strong men into battle.

Open your Bible and read Judges 7:1–7 or tell the story up to this point in your own words.

- What did God tell Gideon to do?
- Did Gideon's army get smaller or bigger?

• How many men did Gideon have to fight the battle?

Gideon wasn't sure he could lead the battle, but God thought differently. That's why he's God! God was in control the whole time. He knew a smaller army would be just the right size to do the job.

Finish the story with Judges 7:16–21.

• Were Gideon and his 300 men enough?
• What happened to the enemy? *(They ran away.)*

Think about it. Gideon's small army was just the right size to topple the powerful Midianites.

You might think you're young and small and not very powerful. What if I told you that God sees great things in you? God has a plan. And in God's plan, a little goes a long way! Trust in him to give you the confidence to win the day. In God's eyes you're just the right size to be his helper.

Bow heads in prayer. **Dear God, in so many little ways, help me to do great things for you. In Jesus' name, amen.**

Hummmmmm

On Your Mark

Bible Truth: We can accomplish tasks when we have faith and trust in God.

Bible Verse: I am sure that the One who began a good work in you will carry it on until it is completed (Philippians 1:6).

Godprint: Confidence

Get Set

Grab Bag: Bible, bag of dime store kazoos, a lap tray, bag of shelled peanuts, blindfold

If you prefer, you can make simple kazoos from empty toilet tissue rolls. Wrap a square of waxed paper over one end and secure it with a rubber band. Children will place the open end of the tube against their mouths and hum. Plastic hair combs work just as well when wrapped in waxed paper. They also tickle the lips as they work!

GO!

Who'd like to join me in humming the tune of *Jesus Loves Me*? Take out the bag of kazoos from your grab bag. **I'll join you!** Distribute the kazoos. **Ready? With a kazoo all you need to do is hum to make it work. Go ahead and give it a try.** Let the music begin!

After a while, stop playing. **That was pretty confident playing. I think our congregation enjoyed it too. Thank you.** Collect the kazoos and put them aside.

- What are some other things that you're confident about doing?
- Are there things you do better today than when you were little?

Pull the lap tray from your grab bag and place it on your lap. **God is happy when we learn new things and grow confident. Today's Scripture tells us, however, that our confidence can only take us so far. God wants us to place our faith and trust in him—first.** Open your Bible and read Philippians 1:6. **We must depend on God before and above all things.**

Take out the peanuts from your grab bag. Spread a handful on your lap tray. **Now if you feel** confident clearing the supper dishes from the table at home raise both hands. Look at all the raised hands. **Now I need only the best, most confident "table clearer" in all the land!** Pick your volunteer. Ask permission to blindfold him or her. **Now, Mr./Ms. Tableclearer, on the count of three clear my tray of all the peanuts. Remember, not one, not some…but all the peanuts. Do you think you can do that?** Pause for a response. **Good! Here we go. On the count of three, clear the table.** Start the count. **One…** quietly lift the tray and have the peanuts fall back into your grab bag…**two…three!** Watch as your volunteer sweeps wildly at an empty tray!

Remove the blindfold from your volunteer. **Hmm. The table was already clear! Sometimes the job is not what we think it is. Sometimes we need a little help knowing what we're supposed to do.** Give your volunteer a warm hug for being a good sport.

Ask a volunteer to read Philippians 1:6.

• According to this verse, what will God do in us?
• Does God ever quit before the job is done?

When we depend only on ourselves, it's like going through life wearing a blindfold. We think we see the whole picture but we're really in the dark. We can accomplish more—in confidence!—when we have faith and trust in God. God is working in you to make you more and more like him. When you face a tough job, trust God to be with you.

Bow heads to pray. **Let's pray. Dear God, bless us and help us place our hope in you. In Jesus' name, amen.**

Knock, Knock

On Your Mark

Bible Truth: Jesus wants to have a relationship with us.

Bible Verse: Here I am! I stand at the door and knock. If any of you hears my voice and opens the door, I will come in and eat with you. And you will eat with me (Revelation 3:20).

Godprint: Faith

Get Set

Grab bag: Bible, a piece of wood (or doorknocker), pizza-flavored chips poured into a small, clean pizza box

Note: As children settle down on the day of your talk, have a member of the congregation quietly walk up and remove your grab bag.

GO!

Knock. Knock.
Pause for children to respond.
Who's there?
Juicy.
Juicy who?
Juicy which way Mr./Ms. (mention your volunteer accomplice by name) **went? He's/She's made off with my grab bag!** Shake a finger and frown at your volunteer as he or she sheepishly returns the bag. Place it safely back by your side.

Let's try another joke. This time let's invite the congregation to join us.

Knock. Knock.
Who's there?
Pizza.
Pizza who?
Pete's a great name but I prefer Pastor/Mr./Ms. (state your name).

Groans all around! Today's Scripture verse talks about a knock—not the joke kind—but the real kind when knuckles rap against a door. Take the wood from your grab bag and knock on wood.

• How quickly do you run to the door when there's a knock or ring?
• How quickly if it's the pizza man? (Very quickly!)

Open your Bible to Revelation 3:20. Ask a strong reader to read the verse aloud.

• When Jesus knocks, what does he want us to do?
• What do you think it would be like to sit down and have supper with Jesus?

Jesus tells us that he stands at the door and knocks. Knock on the wood again. But if your house is anything like mine it's a pretty busy place. The TV is on, and the computer is clicking away, and the dog is barking and there's plenty of arguing from brothers or sisters who don't always get along.

Knock on the wood again. I know many of my friends would give up and go home after just a few short knocks. They'd figure I just wasn't home. Or worse, they'd think I just didn't care enough to answer the door.

A final knock. But Jesus keeps knocking. Jesus wants in—to your heart! He wants for us to turn away from our sins and to open our hearts to his love and salvation. Praise him! With the help of the Holy Spirit we can hear Jesus' voice through all the noise in our busy lives.

Knock. Knock.
Who's there?
Jesus.
Jesus who?
Jesus, the Savior of the world would like to eat supper with you. Pizza delivery! Slide out the pizza box from your grab bag. Open the box and have children help themselves to the pizza-flavored chips.

Hold up your Bible. Remember that Jesus is nearer to you than your own front door. Listen for his knock and invite him in to stay.

Bow heads for prayer. Dear Jesus, thank you for coming to us and knocking on the doors of our hearts. Make us glad to open the door and let you in. Amen.

Knot What They Expected

On Your Mark

Bible Truth: We can trust Jesus at all times.

Bible Story: Jesus calms the storm (Mark 4:35–39).

Godprint: Trust

Get Set

Grab Bag: Bible, comb or brush, flexible straws, water spray bottle, tissues

Just before you begin, dampen your hair with a refreshing spritz from the water spray bottle.

GO!

Take the comb out of your grab bag and tidy up your hair. **I had to leave the house in such a hurry this morning that I forgot to blow dry my hair.** Put the finishing touches on your hair and put the comb away.

Take the straws from the grab bag. **Let's see if I can invent a portable blow dryer for "hurry up!" times such as the one I experienced this morning.** Place the straw in your mouth and use the flexible elbow to point the long end up toward your forehead. Blow-dry your bangs!

Wow. It works. I'm sure to make a million bucks! Who would like to give my new dryer a try? Hand out the straws and give willing hands (or heads) a spray from your water bottle. Have children blow into their straws to dry their hands. (Note: Even though breath contains moisture, much of the water will evaporate from hands—unless, of course, your children are dribblers!)

In today's Scripture, the followers of Jesus were on a boat ride. But it was not the calm and peaceful journey they expected. They were getting very, very wet. Read Mark 4:35–37 or ask a volunteer to help you.

Splish. Splosh. I think the men in the boat could have used our blow dryers! Continue the reading with Mark 4:38.

We also hear how fear tied up the trust our travelers had in the power of Jesus to keep them safe.

• What things make you afraid?
• What can Jesus do for you the next time "tummy knots" grab hold of you?

As children share their thoughts to your questions, tie a knot in the middle of your straw. Have the children do the same. Lend a hand where needed or seek a helper from the congregation. **There is little doubt that tummy knots made the disciples seasick. Those fear "knots" made them unable to trust Jesus. Give your knotted blow dryers a try and see what I mean.** The dryers will not work.

My point? Do your best not to let fear rule by day—or by sea. Trust in Jesus. Remember you are precious to him, and something so precious is worth protecting.

Finish the reading with Mark 4:39.

• How did Jesus make the storm stop?
• What do you think the disciples learned about trusting Jesus?

Now undo the knot in your straw, straighten the straw out a bit and let's give this another try. Success! **We're back in business!** Collect the straws and have children bow their heads in prayer.

Dear God, please talk and walk and play with us every day. We trust you to love and protect us. In Jesus' name, amen.

Lost and Found

On Your Mark

Bible Truth: We can return to God's loving arms, even when we stray.

Bible Story: The Prodigal Son (Luke 15:11–24)

Godprint: Responsibility

Get Set

Grab Bag: Bible, one glove and one mitten, a "Lost and Found" sign

GO!

I remember as a child going with my mother to school on the most important day of the year—Teacher Conference Day! I waited in the hallway as my teacher told my mother everything there was to know about me. Tilt your head and smile broadly. I assure you it was all good news!

What I remember most about that day were the long tables the school janitor had set up in the hallway by the office. Piled high on the tables were boxes filled with shirts, jackets, hats, lunch bags and small toys. Reach into your grab bag and pull out the glove and the mitten. Put them on. Oh, and one box held "onesies"—one-of-a-kind mittens and gloves. Millions of them! The sign taped to the table read, (pull out your sign from the grab bag for the children to read) "Lost and Found."

• How does it feel to find a missing hat, glove or book?
• Why is it so easy to lose things…and so hard to find them?

Open your Bible to Luke 15:11. Our Scripture today is about a young man who found himself pretty much in the "Lost and Found" box. He wanted to be a "onesie" and do his own thing. The problem was he didn't know he was lost! Seeking fun and the good life, this young man takes his share of his father's money and leaves home.

Read Luke 15:11–14. Oh, no. The party's over. This young man is in a real pickle.

• With no money what do you think our young friend will do?
• How do you think this young man felt when he found himself alone with no money?
• Who would you go to for help if you were lost?

Read Luke 15:15, 16. **Pig chow! But not even this food was his to eat. Help!**

Read Luke 15:17–19. **Finally our young friend sees that he's very, very lost. It's no fun being a "onesie." He knew he had made some bad choices, and he was ready to take responsibility for what he'd done. Penniless and hungry, he climbs out of the "Lost" box and heads for the "Found" box, the home of his caring, loving father.**

• Do you think the young man's father will open his home and heart to his runaway son? Or will he be angry?

Finish the reading with Luke 15:20–24. **Fire up the grill and put on the hamburgers! It's barbecue time to help celebrate a son who was once lost but now is found.** Close your Bible.

Jesus tells us this story so that we know that no matter how far away from God we roam, God wants us home. He loves us. When we run away from him and his holy ways, God sits on the front porch with the light on, waiting for our return. When we admit that we've messed up, he's ready to welcome us back. Let's pray to our Father now.

Pause for prayer. **Dear God, we know that we mess up sometimes and wander away from you. Help us to return to your rightful ways. Thank you for welcoming us back. In Jesus' name, amen.**

Needlepoint

On Your Mark

Bible Truth: We praise God for the wonderful world he made.

Bible Verse: In the beginning, God created the heavens and the earth (Genesis 1:1).

Godprint: Worship

Get Set

Grab Bag: Bible, tennis ball, soft-needled pine boughs

GO!

Ask children to hold up their hands and wiggle their fingers. **Who would like to tell me what hands can do?** Pause as children respond.

All that! Let's play a round of patty-cake to celebrate hands. Demonstrate the motions with a volunteer. (Make it simple for your children: clap, pat one hand to one hand, clap, pat the other hand, clap, pat with both hands, end with a final clap.) Then ask children to turn to a neighbor and repeat.

> Pat-a-cake, pat-a-cake, baker's man,
> Bake me a cake as fast as you can.
> Roll it, and prick it, and mark it with a "B,"
> And put it in the oven for Baby and me!

Play until your younger children get the "hand of it" and then clap your hands as a signal to end play. **Very well done!** Hold up your hands again. **Would you agree that I have good-looking hands?** Pause for a nod or two. **Why just the other day I got a call from "Better Homes and Hands" to come and model for them. I only wish I had the time! But even good-looking hands can only do so much.**

Sometimes I have an itch way back here (reach over your shoulder and try to scratch your back). **But no matter how hard I try, my hand just can't reach it.** (A compassionate child just might rise to lend you a hand!) Reach inside your grab bag and remove the tennis ball. **I'd love it, too, if every time I played tennis the ball would fly over the net and score a point. But most times, it just ends up flying over the net and into the parking lot!**

• What things do you have trouble doing with your hands? Tying shoelaces? Buttoning a shirt? Do you sometimes wish your hands were twice their size or teeny-tiny small?

Yes, my hands can only do so much. But with my hands I *can* open the Word of God and read the wonderful things he has done with *his* hands. The Book of Genesis tells us that God made the world. Open your Bible to Genesis 1. Ask a volunteer to read Genesis 1:1. (If you prefer, read more of the creation story, highlighting the days of creation.)

• What does this verse say God made?
• Tell me what God made when he made the heavens and the earth? *(Children may respond with all sorts of answers from creation. Light, water, sky, animals, trees, etc.)*
• God could have made Earth a so-so place. Gray skies, gray trees, gray playgrounds. But he didn't. What does that say about God's love for us?

Take the pine boughs from your grab bag and let children feel the soft texture of the needles. **We're in good hands with the God who made the oceans and the trees and the skies and the bees. This week let your fingers do the talking to remind you of God's awesome creation.** Ask children to hold the pine boughs high and wave them gently. Children who do not have branches can raise one hand and repeat after you.

Start with the thumb. **God does amazing things.** Add a second finger. **God is powerful.** Add a third finger. **God created the world.** Add a fourth finger. **We worship God.** Add a fifth finger. **Let's worship God…with gladness!** Have children wave their hands and pine boughs in gladness.

Bow heads to pray. **Heavenly Father, we thank you for our hands and hearts and lives and the wonderful world we live in.** Have children join you in shouting with gladness. **Aaaaaamen!**

Paper Clip Prayers

On Your Mark

Bible Truth: God wants us to pray for each other.

Bible Verse: At all times, pray by the power of the Spirit. Pray all kinds of prayers.... Always keep on praying for all of God's people (Ephesians 6:18).

Godprint: Prayerfulness

Get Set

Grab Bag: Bible, large colorful paper clips, paper plate, pencil

Ahead of time, use the markers to draw colorful rainbow rings on the inside "circle" of the paper plate.

GO!

God tells us that we are to pray about everything. When we feel wonderful (place your thumbs on your cheeks, wiggle your fingers and smile!) **or when tears fall** (run your pointer fingers down from your eyes). **Whether it's a big thing or a small thing—like the hamster is on the loose and stuck behind the refrigerator—again! God is never too busy to lend us his almighty ear.** Ask a volunteer to read Ephesians 6:18.

- When should we pray?
- What should we pray for?
- How can prayer make you feel better?

Think of someone who can use a prayer right now. We'll understand if your prayer needs to be a silent one, quietly tucked inside your heart.

- Would anyone like to share a prayer request for someone special?

Listen to your children's responses. As you do, reach into your grab bag and remove the bright, colorful paper plate you made ahead of time and the paper clips. With each prayer request or praise have children slide on a paper clip to surround the paper plate rim with colorful paper clip prayers.

We know that God hears all prayers. Big or small. Very important or important only to us. When we pray, God listens. He sees all the colors of our thoughts and feelings.

Grab the pencil from your grab bag and poke it up through the bottom of the plate at the center. Then hold the pencil firmly and give the plate a twirl. See the prayer colors blur into one color. **You can make your own paper clip prayer wheel at home. Each time you pray, add a clip. At the end of the week give it a spin and see how God's love colors them all, no matter what their size or shape. Wait, watch, and listen, and let God surprise you with his answer!**

Pray as a group. **Dear God, we leave the hurt and needs of others in your strong hands. We love you and thank you for listening. In Jesus' name, amen.**

Pass the Peas, Please

On Your Mark

Bible Truth: God blesses us when we look to him for strength.

Bible Verse: Let us not become tired of doing good. At the right time we will gather a crop if we don't give up (Galatians 6:9).

Godprint: Perseverance

Get Set

Grab Bag: Bible, water spray bottle, three flower seed packets labeled "peas," "turnips" and "lettuce," eggshell planters (see instructions below)

Ahead of time, make eggshell planters by cracking raw eggs in half. Pour the contents into a bowl and refrigerate for omelets tomorrow morning! Rinse the shell halves and fill with spoonfuls of potting soil. Use bold, permanent markers to draw happy faces on the eggs. Set the eggshell planters into carton halves for transport inside your grab bag.

GO!

Gardens are amazing gifts from God—gifts that keep giving and giving!

• Does your family plant a vegetable garden in the spring?
• What are your favorite veggies come harvest time?

Open the Bible and read Galatians 6:9.

• What does this verse say about giving up?

Carefully pull out the eggshell planters from your grab bag. **Let's plant a mini-garden right now and see what crop our "heads" can put together!** Tear open the bag of "pea" seeds. Hand the four or five children nearest you each a pea seed.

Mmm, tasty peas! Let's plant our "Ps" first. Have the first group of children press the pea seeds gently into the soil of a number of eggshell planters. Come summer our "Ps" will yield <u>P</u>erseverance and <u>P</u>rayerful <u>P</u>raises (emphasize the P sounds) if we don't give up on following the example of Jesus.

Open the "turnip" seed packet. Now we're ready to plant our "turnips."

• When is the best time to "turn up" to help others?
• Why does Jesus want us to help friends and family?

Good! For bushels of goodness and grace we must *turn up* at church, *turn up* when others need to hear the good news of Jesus and *turn up* to serve others. Finally, tear open the "lettuce" seed packet and have the last group of children plant. Helpful hint: Lettuce seeds are tiny. Have children moisten their fingers and dip them inside the seed packet.

Every garden needs fresh lettuce. *Let us* be truthful and faithful to Jesus. *Let us* always encourage and love one another. And *let us* never forget to ask God's help in doing good. After all, he is the master gardener! Have the youngest child in your group use the water bottle to spritz the newly planted seeds. Set aside the egg carton next to your grab bag. Promise your children that you will place the carton in a sunny window at home or church and bring their "heads" back when they start sprouting. A sunny window is the perfect place for your seeds to rise in the gentle rays of the Son.

Finally, read Galatians 6:7 The Bible tells us that we get what we plant. Before we leave today, let's squash some ugly weeds in our home garden that are sure to grow. Clap with me each time you hear the word *squash*. Ready? *Squash* (clap) unkindness. *Squash* (clap) selfishness. *Squash* (clap) hurtful words. Offer a round of applause. Good job, gardeners!

Bow heads in prayer. Dear God, you want us to keep on doing good and following your way. Help us to keep on going in the way that you lead. Amen.

S.A.T. Test

On Your Mark

Bible Truth: We can learn from Jesus how to follow him.

Bible Story: Jesus and his disciples went on their way. Jesus came to a village where a woman named Martha lived. She welcomed him into her home. She had a sister named Mary. Mary sat at the Lord's feet listening to what he said. But Martha was busy with all the things that had to be done. She came to Jesus and said, "Lord, my sister has left me to do the work by myself. Don't you care? Tell her to help me!" "Martha, Martha," the Lord answered. "You are worried and upset about many things. But only one thing is needed. Mary has chosen what is better. And it will not be taken away from her" (Luke 10:38–42).

Godprint: Discipleship

Get Set

Grab Bag: Bible, a seat cushion, lightweight aluminum pie plates, penny whistles

GO!

Growing up in a big and busy house there were always chores to do. Take out the seat cushion from your grab bag and sit on it. Place your hands behind your neck and let out a big sigh. Relax! **And better that a tornado come stormin' by or an earthquake swallow the house whole than my mother come home to find me sitting and watching TV!**

But in today's Scripture reading we hear that sometimes sitting around beats out chores any day! Turn to the congregation. **What do you think about that, Mom?** Have children turn to the congregation and give a thumbs up. One or two moms may very well respond with a definite thumbs down! **Moms are right. There is enough time in our days to clear the table, feed the puppy, take out the garbage and do our homework. But Jesus tells us that each day we must find time to listen to the important things God says in his Word.**

- What busy things take up your time Monday through Friday? *(Breakfast, walking to school, feeding the goldfish, school work, soccer, piano lessons.)*
- If all the pieces to your day fit into a puzzle, where would the "pray and talk to Jesus" piece go?

Ask a willing child to read Luke 10:38, 39. **Sisters! Mary and Martha lived together as a family.**

• What are two really good things about having a sister or brother?

• What is one thing that your sister or brother does very well?

• Do you always get along with your brother or sister?

Read Luke 10:40. **Oops. I feel a storm a-brewin'.** Take the pie plates and penny whistles from your grab bag and distribute them. **Let's hear an angry storm between sisters.** Have children bang plates and whistle—loudly. **Oh, my ears!** After a bit, ask children to drop the noisemakers back into your grab bag.

• How was the struggle between Mary and Martha a lot like what you feel at home?

• How would Jesus like you to treat your brother or sister?

Read Luke 10:41, 42. **Jesus listened patiently to Martha. He loved that she was busy preparing a nice dinner for him. But sometimes dinner must wait. Jesus had important things to say that Martha needed to hear.**

• What is Jesus telling Martha in this verse?

Mary chose what was better. Sitting at the feet of Jesus, Mary heard Jesus' message of love and the power of his words as God's Son. And now we can too!

Let's pray. Bow heads in prayer. **Dear God, help us to be still and listen to what you have to say. Thank you for telling us about yourself. Help us to tell others about you too. Amen.**

Seven Ups

On Your Mark

Bible Truth: God helps us to do the work he gives us.

Bible Verse: [Jesus] was sitting with the teachers. He was listening to them and asking them questions. Everyone who heard him was amazed at how much he understood. They were also amazed at his answers (Luke 2:46, 47).

Godprint: Confidence

Get Set

Grab Bag: Bible, a can of 7UP® soda

GO!

Good morning! Let's check out our confidence meter today.

• Tell about a happy memory of a time when you did something very, very well.
• What would you build if you had all the confidence in the world?

I'd like you to give me two reasons why you got up to come to church this morning. Pause for children to respond. **Mom made you come? So did Dad? Well, hurray for moms and dads.** Flash a thumbs up at the congregation. **Those are two very good reasons!**

Jesus came to earth for a very good reason too—it was to do his Father's work. Even as a young boy Jesus was confident in telling the world of the supreme goodness and power of his Father. We can be confident in the work God wants us to do. Have a volunteer read Luke 2:41–47 aloud.

• What did Jesus do that was so amazing in this story?
• How did Jesus show confidence in this story?

Reach into your grab bag and hold up the soda can. **We can use this can to remind us to be confident in the role God the Father has for us. Let's see how many "ups" we can come "up" with! We can...**

Stand *up*! Just as Jesus did in his Father's house, the temple. He spoke boldly about what he knew to be the truth to men much older than he was. Have children stand up, raise their hands in the air and shout, "Stand up for Jesus!" **That's one!**

Speak *up*! Don't ever be afraid to ask questions about the wonderful things of God. Scripture tells us that Jesus asked many questions in the temple. Have children shout, "Up with the Lord!" **Stand up and speak up. That's two.**

Look *up*! To those who can help you see God. Jesus looked up to his mom and dad and the temple teachers even though he was the Son of God. After all, he was only 12 years old, and he knew God wanted him to respect his parents. Have children turn to the congregation and blow kisses to their parents.

• Do Mom and Dad have all the answers you need? *(Sure they do. They're wonderful!)*

Stand up, speak up and look up. That's three.

Lift *up!* Our prayers to God. Jesus prayed to his Father. Mary and Joseph may have done the same when they feared that their son was lost. Stand up, speak up, look up and lift up. That's four.

Eyes on me now as we pray. Listen for three more "ups" as we pray.

Pause as children join hands. **Dear God, thank you for sending Jesus. Remind us to take *up*** (hold up the soda can), **shake *up*** (shake up the soda can) **and wake *up* our confidence each morning to do what God knows is best. In Jesus' name, amen.**

Stand up, speak up, look up, lift up, take up, shake up, and wake up. That's seven!

And now time's up! Before dismissing your children say, **Please join me outside church after service this morning.** Give the soda can a final hearty shake. **When we open the can, we'll watch as it shakes up and wakes up with a hissing fizz of confidence!**

Take a Brake

On Your Mark

Bible Truth: God wants us to honor him in our attitudes and actions.

Bible Verse: But the fruit the Holy Spirit produces is love, joy and peace. It is being patient, kind, and good. It is being faithful and gentle and have control of oneself (Galatians 5:22, 23).

Godprint: Self-control

Get Set

Grab Bag: Bible, small toy cars, red paper circle cut from construction paper

GO!

Take a toy car from your grab bag and play with it as your children settle in for today's talk. **It's great fun to play with toy cars.** Make the car do circles and "spin out" in your palm. **When I was your age I would take my cars and have them "accidentally" fall off tabletops or from steps in the backyard—even topple into a pail of soapy water. How do you play with your cars?** Pause as children respond, then raise your palm and have the toy car fall "out of control" back into the grab bag. **Such fun! But we know that with real cars it takes self-control to make sure this never happens.**

• Was it hard the first time you rode your bike? How long did it take before you could ride well?

The Holy Spirit, who is God's special messenger, wants us to control our behavior so we act with patience, kindness and gentleness. Open your Bible and read Galatians 5:22, 23 or ask a volunteer to read.

• According to these verses, how does God want us to act?
• What does "self-control" mean?
• What is one of the first things you notice about a friend with self-control? Is she kind and gentle?

Let's gear up now to practice a bit of self-control. Reach into your grab bag and take out all the toy cars you brought with you as well as the red construction paper circle. Ask children to back up a bit and then place the red circle on the floor by your feet. Distribute the cars to children.

We'll take turns seeing which of our cars rolls closest to the red parking "spot" without actually touching it. Practice self-control and wait your turn. If another car bumps yours away from the spot, don't "brake" down! That's the way the game is played. You'll get another chance the next go around.

If your group is large for the number of cars you have, separate your children into teams and determine a "driver" for each team. Play for two or three minutes and then collect the cars. I'll leave the cars and the parking spot here. After church those who didn't get to play—and who showed great self-control and patience!—can come up and give it a go.

Hold up a car and draw the attention back to you. Kids on board! Remember, out-of-control behavior doesn't work in a car, when riding a bike or when skateboarding. Just imagine skiing down a snowy hill without control! For all these things you must be in control.

Let's ask God's help to stay in control so the Holy Spirit can do his thing in us. Pause for prayer. Dear God, help us to be loving and kind and patient and still have fun at the same time. In Jesus' name, amen.

Take Out the Trash

On Your Mark

Bible Truth: Knowing Jesus is the best thing in the world.

Bible Verse: Even more, I consider everything to be nothing compared to knowing Christ Jesus my Lord. To know him is the best thing of all. Because of him I have lost everything. But I consider all of it to be garbage so I can get to know Christ (Philippians 3:8).

Godprint: Conviction

Get Set

Grab Bag: Bible, paper lunch bag, gold necklace, hand-held electronic game, a kid's favorite video or DVD, $5.00 bill, marker, small trashcan

GO!

Set the trashcan beside you and welcome your children as they arrive. **There is a story about an old lady who searched her home to find the best place to hide her beautiful jewelry.** Reach into your grab bag and pull out the gold necklace.

And where do you think she finally decided to put it? Listen to all guesses. **Close!** Take the paper lunch bag from your grab bag. **The lady of the house decided to place all her jewelry in a brown paper lunch bag and set it in her cupboard.** Open the bag and drop in the necklace.

• What things do you own that mean a lot to you?
• What makes each piece valuable?
• Where do you keep things that are valuable?

I have a few other things here in my grab bag that I think you'd consider worth having. Reach into your bag and take out the hand-held electronic game. **What do you think of this?** Have children take a look, then drop it inside the lunch bag. Follow this with the video or DVD. Finally, hold up the $5.00 bill. **What about this? Is money something you consider valuable?** Drop the money inside the lunch bag and roll the bag closed. Set the bag aside.

On with the story! Now you'll never guess what happened the afternoon our dear old lady grabbed a bucket and brush and started her spring cleaning. Out from the cupboard

came the old cereal and the stale cookies. Out from the cupboard came the sticky sprinkles and rock-hard sugar. And out came the little brown lunch bag. After a whisk-and-a-wash-and-a scrub-a-dub-dub, the lady picked up the old, dusty lunch bag (*use the marker to write the word* TRASH *on the front of the lunch sack*) **and threw it away!** *Drop the lunch bag into the trashcan. Watch the wide-eyed reaction of your children.*

Open your Bible to Philippians 3:8 and read the verse.

• What does this verse say is the best thing of all?

We learn a valuable lesson from our story today. From a prison cell in Rome, the Apostle Paul tells us that all the jewelry, money and fortune of this world mean nothing to him. In fact, it's all garbage compared to knowing Jesus. Yes, garbage! By putting his faith in Christ Jesus, Paul gained everything worth having.

Remove the lunch bag from the trashcan and put it back in your grab bag. **Jesus doesn't want us to go home and throw away our jewelry. But he does want us to know that we gain the best treasure of all when we believe in him. Live rich in the love of Christ!**

Bow heads in prayer. **Dear God, help us to hold on to what we cannot lose. Help us to remember that knowing you is the best thing in the world. In Jesus' name, amen.**

The Lilies and Birds . . .
and the Ladybugs!

On Your Mark

Bible Truth: Rely on God completely because he is trustworthy.

Bible Verse: Think about the ravens. They don't plant or gather crops...But God feeds them. You are worth much more than birds...Think about how the lilies grow. They don't work or make clothing...Not even Solomon in all of his glory was dressed like one of those flowers (Luke 12:24–27).

Godprint: Trust

Get Set

Grab bag: Bible, a silk lily, an orange, 8-inch red tissue paper or napkin square, black marker, colorful round stickers

GO!

Spring is a joyous time of year to take a walk. Birds chirp, flowers sprout and ladybugs do little dances of happiness! See if an energetic child would like to stand and perform a dance of happiness for the group.

What energy! Thank you. In today's Scripture, Jesus takes a long walk with his friends. Soon they come upon a hillside. Much to everyone's delight Jesus stops to look upon the birds of the air and the lilies growing in the warm, dark soil. There might even have been a ladybug—or two—enjoying the day as well! Take the square of red tissue paper from the bag. Use the marker to make a happy lady-bug face on the side facing you. Draw two happy antennae.

Read Luke 12:24.

• What is a raven? *(A bird.)*
• Why did Jesus talk about the birds?

Jesus tells the crowd to take a good look at the birds. No worried birds here. God takes

care of bird wings and feathers and empty bird tummies. Hand the sticker sheet to several children and have them put some happy dots on the ladybug tissue paper square.

Read Luke 12:27. Pull up the silk lily from your grab bag. Caress the cheeks of several children with it. **Under a bright sky Jesus looks at the loveliness of the lilies. Jesus tells his friends that the pretty lily petals are more beautiful than King Solomon's finest robe. God, the Father, cares for flowers.** Put the lily down and pick up the tissue paper. Twist the corners of the lady bug paper to form a small dome. Take an orange from your grab bag and place it on the floor. Drop the ladybug dome on top of the orange and gently give the orange a push. Watch the wobbly walk of a happy ladybug! If you prefer, use an eight-inch green square for a happy turtle. Change colors for the happy animal of your choice.

The little birds and the lovely lilies…and even the small dotted wings of a ladybug are under God's protection. How much more can we trust God to care for you and me? Bunches and bunches!

Bow heads in thankful prayer. **Dear God, we are thankful that we can trust you to care for us. In Jesus' name, amen.**

Before children head back to their seats, say, **Ask Mom or Dad to help you make a ladybug to keep at home. A square of paper and a fruit is all you need! Then share its "wobbly" surprise and today's Scripture, Luke 12:24–27, with a friend.**

Kids' Choice Award

On Your Mark

Bible Truth: Because we are created in God's image, we are loved and highly valued.

Bible Verse: Some people brought little children to Jesus. They wanted him to place his hands on the children and pray for them. But the disciples told the people to stop. Jesus said, "Let the little children come to me. Don't keep them away. The kingdom of heaven belongs to people like them" (Matthew 19:13, 14).

Godprint: Preciousness

Get Set

Grab Bag: Bible, a trophy, blue ribbon tags (p. 74), cut apart

If possible, photocopy the ribbon tags on blue paper.

GO!

Jesus loved people. Every day he met people on the road—mothers, fathers, babies, little children. Big and little people all wanted a hug or a blessing from the Son of God.

But one day, Jesus' disciples would not let the children come to visit with Jesus, to sit on his lap or play games. Jesus was just too important for such things. In the disciples' eyes, Jesus didn't have time for noisy, happy children who needed hugs and asked lots of questions. Time was important. Jesus had a schedule to keep.

Hand your Bible to a reader. Read Matthew 19:13, 14.

• What was Jesus' response when the disciples shooed the children away? *(Don't keep them from me.)*
• The children in today's Bible story were very precious to Jesus. How does Jesus feel about you? *(Jesus loves you deeply too.)*

Jesus loves children! Children are not a bother for Jesus. They are important as well as precious creations to him. Choosy children all over the world choose Jesus because his hugs are soft, his hands gentle and his heart burns bright with love for them.

Ask your children for a show of hands. **Who thinks Jesus is #1?** Pause and count hands. **The vote is in.** Reach into your grab bag and pull out the trophy. Ask a child to come forward and hold it high. **The Kids' Choice Award goes to…** Have children perform a drum roll by slapping their legs with their hands. **Jesus!**

Let's talk to our award winner now. Gather for prayer. **Dear Jesus, we are precious to you and for that we are truly thankful. Amen.**

Now let's do a little cheer to celebrate how precious we are to Jesus. Repeat after me.

We choose you	(Children) *We choose you*
No one else will do	(Children) *No one else will do*
Yeaaaaaah, Jesus!	

Before children head back to their seats, take the blue ribbons from your grab bag and pass them out. **Jesus loves the little children! Pin your hopes on him.**

I Love Others

Our relationship with a loving God lets us reach out and love others. We can call on God when people we know need help. God gives us work to do—and then helps us do it. He wants us to show his light to our friends and family. God's love transforms our lives, and he wants us to pass his love on to others. When we reach out to others with kindness, love and prayer, we reflect the light of God's love to the world.

101 Reasons for Faith

On Your Mark

Bible Truth: We can call on God when others need help.

Bible Story: The centurion asked Jesus to heal his servant (Matthew 8:5–10, 13).

Godprint: Prayerfulness

Get Set

Grab Bag: Bible, military fatigues (cap and jacket), a construction paper "purple heart," a paper clip

GO!

Pull out your military cap from the grab bag and put it on. **Today's Scripture talks about a military commander. The Bible tells us he was an army man, the leader of 100 soldiers.** Pull out the military jacket from the grab bag and put it on as well. **We can be sure that when the commander talked, 100 Roman soldiers listened.**

One day this commander wanted to talk to Jesus. Now Romans, especially powerful commanders, did not make it a habit to talk with Jews. And Jesus was a Jew. But the commander's heart was deeply troubled. Remove the "purple heart" and the paper clip from your bag. Thread the clip through the buttonhole in your jacket or simply "pin" the paper heart to your lapel. **The commander with the troubled heart searched the streets of Capernaum, here, there and everywhere for Jesus. Let's look for Jesus, too.** If the size of your group permits, ask the kids to stand up and follow you as you walk around a bit, searching. If you don't have space for everyone to walk, have kids put their hands to their foreheads to shade their eyes as they look all around.

Once everyone is settled again, open your Bible and read Matthew 8:5, 6 or have a good reader do it.

Oh my. The commander's servant was sick. That's why he was looking for Jesus. The commander had heard of Jesus' miracles to cure the sick. He knew Jesus could heal his sick servant.

• When have you prayed for someone to feel better?

Read Matthew 8:7-9. Jesus was ready to go and find this sick man. But the commander stopped him. His heart was sad because his servant was sick, but it was also full of faith. He knew that Jesus had the power to just "say a word" and his servant's pain would come to an end. This leader of 100 men had a powerful faith in Jesus' power to heal. Finish today's story by reading Matthew 8:10, 13.

What power! Our Roman commander had 100 reasons to live a life without Jesus. And each one of them respected him. But none of these reasons could heal his servant. Neither his power, nor title, nor money could do anything for the sick man. Only the power of one could heal. Jesus!

• God hears us when we pray for others. He knows your voice! When can you talk to him today before the sun sets?

Let's make prayer our "badge of honor." In prayer we can use our faith in God to help others. Praise God for the gift of faith. Bow heads to pray. Dear God, thank you for the gift of faith. Help us follow the army man's example and put faith in your Son's power to hear, help and heal. In Jesus' name, amen.

Batteries for a Lifetime

On Your Mark

Bible Truth: God helps us to do his work in the world.

Bible Verse: "Then Jesus…said, 'All authority in heaven and on earth has been given to me. So you must go and make disciples of all nations. Baptize them in the name of the Father and of the Son and of the Holy Spirit. Teach them to obey everything I have commanded you. And you can be sure that I am always with you, to the very end'" (Matthew 28:18–20).

Godprint: Commitment

Get Set

Grab Bag: Bible, a portable CD player with CD and headphones

Take the batteries out of the CD player and remove the battery plate or cover. Put the batteries and plate cover in the grab bag.

GO!

As your children settle in pull out the CD player and earphones from your grab bag. Connect the earphones and turn on the CD player. Hold the CD player in such a way that children can see that the batteries are missing. Frown! Take off the headphones and keep pressing the "on" button. **Humph. I can't get my CD player to work. No matter how many times I press the "on" button, it just won't play.** If your children don't immediately notice that the batteries are missing, set the CD player on the floor in front of you and have them examine it closely.

Ah, batteries! Rummage through your grab bag and take out the batteries and plate cover. Put the batteries in and put on the cover. Turn on the player and have the children take turns listening to the music through your headphones.

Well, that's better. We just needed a little energy to get things going. Put the CD player and headphones back in the bag.

After Jesus' death on the cross his followers were afraid. They weren't sure if soldiers would come and hurt them too. In fact, they had doubts whether everything Jesus had

told them was really true. Their energy and commitment were running low. Read Matthew 28:16–19 or ask a strong reader to help you.

• Who did the disciples see on the mountain? *(Jesus.)*
• What did Jesus tell the disciples to do? *(Go tell the world about him.)*

Jesus knew his disciples had some doubts. Was it all true? Would they be able to do the job? Jesus let them know they could keep their energy going. He wanted them to tell the Good News to the world. And that's what they did. As the disciples traveled to tell others about Jesus, he was with them every step of the way. How do I know? Jesus tells me so. Read Matthew 28:20. And *always* means always!

Don't let your energy run low. Don't let fear "unplug" you from God. Jesus' batteries last a lifetime. Stay connected!

Bow heads to pray. **Dear God, thank you for allowing Jesus to live in our hearts. Help us tell others all about him. In Jesus' name, amen.**

Tozes and Nozes

On Your Mark

Bible Truth: God wants us to tell the truth.

Bible Verse: Don't lie to each other (Colossians 3:9).

Godprint: Honesty

Get Set

Grab Bag: Bible, a towel

GO!

Pull the towel from your grab bag, roll it and drape it around your neck. Then perform a few toe touches and reach-for-the-sky stretches. Use your towel to wipe your face and let out a long breath. **Stand up, everyone. Join me and let's exercise a bit to start off our time today.** A few jumping jacks should get everyone warmed up.

Now for the real deal! Repeat and do what I do. Ready? This is my nose. Point to your nose. Pause as children touch their noses. **These are my toes.** Reach down and touch your toes. Pause as children touch their toes. **Excellent!** Repeat the process, pointing again to your nose and then toes, nose and toes, until your children perform in a steady rhythm. **Good job. I have a very athletic bunch this morning!**

Now that we're all warmed up, let's have some fun. Repeat and do what I do. This is my elbow. Point to your *head!* **This is my arm.** Point to your *leg!* **These are my ears.** Rub your *stomach.* **Now let's put all our actions together.**

This is my nose. *Touch nose.*
These are my toes. *Touch toes.*
This is my elbow. *Touch head.*
This is my arm. *Touch leg.*
These are my ears. *Rub tummy!*

Children will do their best to follow you. Even older children will have a hard time if you quicken the pace. **That was tricky, wasn't it?** Have the children shake out their giggles and wiggles and then sit down.

• Is this *really* my elbow? (Touch your head.)
• Is this *really* my arm? (Touch your leg.)

We had fun today. Being tricky can be fun. But I'd like to talk about times when being tricky is not fun at all. Have you ever had anyone trick you with a lie? Pause. **When people lie, they pretend not to know the truth. When friends lie they say one thing but mean another. In Colossians, the Bible says, "Don't lie to each other."** This is the first phrase of Colossians 3:9. You may want to have a volunteer read just that phrase from your Bible.

• Why is it wrong to lie? *(Lying hurts others, lying is not what Christ would do and God wants Christ's way to be our way.)*
• How do lies make you unhappy?

Lies are selfish and sinful. Lies push the truth under the bed where nobody can find it.

• Why are friends who tell the truth a blessing from God?

God is holy and perfect. He doesn't lie to us, and he doesn't want us to lie to each other. His love helps us tell the truth. And just like exercise, when we warm up to God our hearts change. They get bigger and better, warmer and brighter!

Bow heads to pray. **Dear God, you made us to need others. Help us to be truthful and honest. In Jesus' name we pray, amen.** Have children put their best foot forward and jog back to their seats.

Have It Your Way

On Your Mark

Bible Truth: God wants us to show his light to our friends.

Bible Verse: "I am the light of the world. Those who follow me will never walk in darkness. They will have the light that leads to life" (John 8:12).

Godprint: Friendliness

Get Set

Grab Bag: Bible, hand mirror, flashlight (9 1/2-inch), three 7-inch balloons—one red, one green and one blue

Cut the stem off each of the balloons. Practice stretching them, each one separately, over the 2-inch lens of the flashlight.

GO!

Reach into your grab bag and take out the flashlight and cut balloons. Place the balloons in your lap and turn on the flashlight. **Light keeps us one step ahead of the darkness. Light keeps us from losing our way.**

- How does a flashlight help on a nighttime adventure?
- Do you sleep better with a night-light in your room? Why?

Jesus tells us he is the light of the world. Read John 8:12 from your Bible.

- According to this verse, what happens to those who follow Jesus?
- How can we show Jesus' light to other people?

Close your eyes for a moment and think of a white light that sparkles and glows very bright. Pause as children imagine. **Open all eyes! Did your light look like the light from my flashlight? Brighter? Wonderful!** Ask a child to come up and place his or her hand over the lens of your flashlight. **Black out! Even the best of lights won't work if it's covered. One way we cover up Jesus' light is with our feelings-of-many-colors.**

Stretch the red balloon over the lens of the flashlight. **Lots of times we "see red" when we don't get what we want. We get angry. We stomp our feet and shout for all to hear.**

• How do you feel when you're the last to get dessert or when a friend doesn't want to play with you?
• Who can show me an angry face? (Take out the mirror from your grab bag and have children take a look.)

Remove the red balloon and replace it with the green one. **When a friend gets a new bike or computer game, do you feel jealous inside, wishing it were yours? Some people call that being "green with envy." Like a sick leaf on a tree, jealousy shrinks loving hearts and makes them smaller. Then we can't show Jesus' light.**

• Jealousy can break up the best of friendships. Why is it important to show your friends that you care more about them than about what they have?

Remove the green balloon and replace it with the blue one. **Sometimes it's not that we care too much but that we care too little! We act "cool blue," not caring about what others feel or need.**

• How does a "cold shoulder" from a teammate on the playground make you feel?

Remove the blue balloon from the lens. Let the clear, bright light shine again for all to see. **Even though we are broken and weak and sometimes want what others have, Jesus' light is always reaching out to us.** Have children grab hold of your flashlight. **Let's grab hold of Jesus' light and allow him to have his way in us. Then he can shine through us so others can come to know Jesus too.**

Join hands and hearts in prayer. **Dear God, thank you for your out-of-this world, light-of-the-world Son, Jesus! May he always shine through us for others to see. Amen.** Have children shout, "I've seen the light!" before returning to their seats.

Hand Some

On Your Mark

Bible Truth: God wants us to be kind and help others as God is kind and helps us.

Bible Story: The servant hurried to meet [Rebekah]. "Please give me a little water from your jar." "Have a drink, sir," she said. She quickly lowered the jar to her hands. And she gave him a drink. After she had given him a drink, she said, "I'll get water for your camels too. I'll keep doing it until they finish drinking" (Genesis 24:17–19).

Godprint: Kindness

Get Set

Grab Bag: Bible, pastel-colored latex glove, flour, a bag of treats

Before church, make a "hand" by filling a supple, pastel-colored latex glove with baking flour. Stretch and double knot the end to tie it off. You can find pastel-colored gloves at a medical supply store. If there isn't a store in your area, lightly fill a clear glove from a commercial kitchen or fast-food restaurant. You may wish to make two "hands" if your group is large.

GO!

• Tell me of a time when you needed an extra hand to help clean your room or finish household chores.

I can think of lots of times when I need a hand too. Let's see. Just yesterday I was mixing a batch of double-fudge brownies. My hands were smudged with flour and I had a prickly itch right here on the top of my nose. Give your nose a rub. **My** (wife, husband, son, daughter) **was very kind to give me a hand and scratch my itchy nose.**

An extra hand is, well, handy! In the Book of Genesis, the Bible tells us that Abraham's servant took a long journey to find a wife for Abraham's son, Isaac. Along the way he met Rebekah, who gave him a helping hand. Open your Bible and read Genesis 24:17–19.

• What did the servant ask for? *(A little water.)*
• What did Rebekah give? *(Water for the servant, plus all his camels.)*

Traveling in a hot, dry desert with 10 cranky camels must have been tiresome. Rebekah recognized the servant's need and watered it!

• How can you tell if someone you know needs a little help with something?
• What are some ways you can be kind or helpful to other people?

Take the glove(s) from your grab bag and hand it (them) to your children.

When your turn comes, give my "hand" a shake. Then share a time you offered a new neighbor or classmate a hand in friendship. Maybe you said a cheery hello to a new boy or girl on your street or sat down to share a snack with someone new at school. Pause and listen to your children share their stories. Then collect the latex hands.

Sometimes we get help and sometimes we give it. Either way, kindness makes it happen. Let's thank God for his kindness now.

Bow heads in prayer. Heavenly Father, help us remember that kindness means never having to say, "I'm too busy to be kind to someone today." In Jesus' name, amen.

You've all been great listeners. Open up the bag of treats. Ask an older volunteer for a helping hand! Please take a piece of candy and then hand some to the other children. Before children head back to their seats hold up the latex hand and say, Anyone care to guess what's inside my "hands?" Because of the soft, spongy feel, glove feels like they're filled with jelly or hand cream. Kindness? Yes...and also baking flour that you have in your kitchen at home. Surprise!

Holy Presents

Bible Truth: God wants us to pass his love on to others.

Bible Verse: You have given him blessings that will last forever. You have made him glad and joyful because you are with him (Psalm 21:6).

Godprint: Love

Get Set

Grab Bag: a gift-wrapped Bible, a clear 1-liter water bottle with cap prepared as directed below, a package of small plastic heart beads that will fit easily inside your bottle

Fill the bottle 1/4 full with Isopropyl rubbing alcohol followed by vegetable oil to within an inch of the top. Once the oil settles, add some glitter and a few drops of food coloring. Give the bottle a shake to mix all of the above.

GO!

My birthday is coming up!

• What makes a birthday present special?
• Which do you like best, giving presents or getting them?

I received an early birthday present this morning. Let's see what it is. Reach into your grab bag and pull out your wrapped Bible. Ask a helper to unwrap it for you.

My Bible! What a thoughtful present. Flip through the Bible pages for your children to see.

Look. It comes with bookmarks, highlighted passages and all my scribbled notes. I suppose some people might call this a "holy present." After all, the Bible is God's Word, holy and true. Today, though, I want to share with you about God's holy *presence*. It sounds a lot like *present*. And God's *presence* is a lot like a *present*.

Hold up your Bible and a piece of the wrapping paper. **God's presence is shiny like this wrapping**

paper and new every morning. And even though it's not a gift you can touch or unwrap, God's presence is a never-ending gift from God to us. Turn to Psalm 21:6 and read the verse aloud.

• What does this verse say God gives us?
• How long will these presents last?

Reach into your grab bag and pull out the bag of heart beads and the water bottle you prepared ahead of time. Give the bottle a shake to mix the settled contents. Hold it in front of you for your children to view.

One of the greatest blessings God gives us is his love. God is love. All love comes from him. When Mom or Dad or Grandma give you a loving hug, it means only one thing: that God hugged them first! God is love. Let's think of the water in this bottle as God's love. Unscrew the cap from the bottle. Ask your children to step forward and take a bead from the open bag and drop it into the bottle. (Beads are choking hazards for young children, so make sure the beads go directly from the bag into the water bottle.) Once the children finish dropping in beads, secure the cap and give the bottle a good shake. **When we live in God's presence, God pours his love and blessings in and around us just like the water in this bottle.** Pause as children watch the sparkling water bubble and flow in and around their suspended "hearts." **We can't see or touch God, but his *presence* and love are all around us all the time. And that's something to be glad about!** Tighten the cap and then pass around the bottle for children to see. After a while put the bottle back in your bag.

So here are five (hold up your hand) **great things to know about God in us.** Have children raise their hands and count off their fingers as they repeat after you.

God is love. *God is love.*
If we love God, he lives in us. *If we love God, he lives in us.*
God's love is a great blessing. *God's love is a great blessing.*
When we love others, we pass on God's love. *When we love others we pass on God's love.*
God is love! *God is love!*

Now knit your fingers together in prayer. Pause. **Dear God, we cannot make ourselves holy. Only you can do that. Thank you for loving and living in us. We love you sooooooo much! In Jesus' name, amen.**

Bubbles

On Your Mark

Bible Truth: When we help others, we reflect God's love.

Bible Story: The Good Samaritan, Luke 10:30–35 and Matthew 25:40. "Anything you did for one of the least important of these brothers or sisters of mine, you did for me."

Godprint: Kindness

Get Set

Grab Bag: Bible, a sheet of bubble wrap, paper crown (p. 90), bubble solution with a wand

GO!

Take the paper crown from your grab bag and place it on your head. Then hold up your Bible. **Kings fill the pages of the Bible. Many had armies, slept in soft beds, ate only the finest foods and wore beautiful and expensive robes.**

• What do you think would make a king happy?
• What would make a king sad?

But King Jesus was different. Jesus' home was wherever people would have him. A loyal band of disciples was his army and his clothes were sturdy, traveling clothes. All this he did so he could talk and walk with everyday people—like you and me!

• What would make King Jesus happy?
• What would make King Jesus sad?

Ask for an older volunteer to step up. Reach into your grab bag and pull out the bubble wrap. Drape it over his or her shoulders as if it were a kingly robe, bubble side out. Place the crown on your volunteer's head.

King Jesus wants us to love each other as we love ourselves. When we hurt our neighbor we also hurt our king. Let's listen to a very sad story with a happy ending. Now each time I read a sad, hurtful thing I'll pause. Then I'll choose two of you to step up and "pop" the king's robe. Ready? Open your Bible and read Luke 10:30a:

Jesus replied, "A man was going down from Jerusalem to Jericho. Robbers attacked him."

Have two children step up and pop the bubble wrap and then sit back down. Continue the reading with Luke 10:30b:

"They stripped off his clothes and beat him."

Have two more children step up and give the robe a pop. Finish the sad parts of the story with more bubble pops for Luke 10:30c:

"Then they went away, leaving him almost dead."

And Luke: 10:31:

"A priest happened to be going down that same road. When he saw the man, he passed by on the other side."

And Luke 10:32:

"A Levite also came by. When he saw the man, he passed by on the other side too."

Oh! So many pops. Our king's robe is looking mighty ragged. But now for the happy ending! Read Luke 10:33:

"But a Samaritan came to the place where the man was. When he saw the man, he felt sorry for him."

Grab the bubble solution from your grab bag, open it and hand it to a child who has not had a turn yet. **Blow some bubbles to replace the ones we popped.** Continue the story (Luke 10:34, 35) pausing for bubbles between verses.

"He went to him, poured olive oil and wine on his wounds and bandaged them. Then he put the man on his own donkey. He took him to an inn and took care of him. The next day, he took out two silver coins. He gave them to the owner of the inn. 'Take care of him,' he said. 'When I return, I will pay you back for any extra expense you may have.'"

Thank your "kingly" volunteer and put away the bubble wrap, crown and bubble solution. **King Jesus tells us: "Anything you did for one of the least important of these brothers or sisters of mine, you did for me"** (Matthew 25:40). **Remember this the next time a brother or friend or neighbor needs help. Be helpers for Jesus and show others that God loves them.**

Gather children in prayer. **Let's pray. Dear God, help us to see Jesus in the people we meet each day. Help us to reflect your love in everything we do. In Jesus' name, amen.**

Crown Pattern-Cut out, Join and Fasten

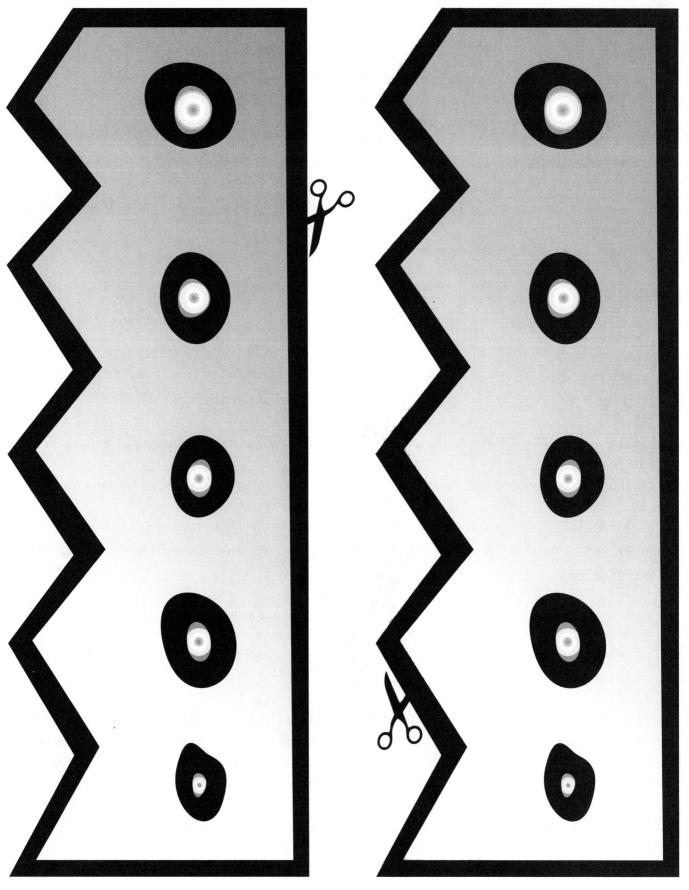

Seasonal Sermons

Christmas. Easter. Pentecost. Your congregation likely plans special ways to observe these important days in the life of the church. Your celebration may even extend over several weeks. In this section, you'll find children's sermons for these seasonal occasions. You'll help children learn that God is worthy of our highest praise, that Jesus' example of humility teaches us how to treat others, that Jesus' resurrection gives us hope for the future. By the gift of his Holy Spirit, God helps us to tell others about Jesus. Rejoice and celebrate!

Goin' Wishin'

On Your Mark

Bible Truth: God is worthy of our highest praise.

Bible Story: Wise men follow the star, Matthew 2:1–11

Godprint: Worship

Get Set

Grab Bag: Bible, shiny foil star, wrapped Christmas presents, a small bed with a toddler doll for Jesus

Ahead of time, set the bed within walking distance from where you sit with your children.

GO!

As children settle in on the day of your talk, reach inside your grab bag and pull out the foil star. **I wish I may, I wish I might, get the wish I wish tonight!** Have children repeat after you.

• What do you think about when you watch a pretty star twinkle in the night sky?

• If you kept your eye on that star, do you think it could lead you on a great adventure? Why or why not?

Our Scripture today talks of a bright and beautiful star in a night sky long ago and many miles from the town of Bethlehem. A few wise men who lived at the time took notice. Night after night they studied the star. Indeed, there must be a reason why this one glowed so bright—a king must be on his way! The wise men packed up Christmas presents and started a great journey toward the star. They wished to meet the new king.

Have children repeat after you. **I wish I may, I wish I might, get the wish I wish tonight!**

Open your Bible and read Matthew 2:1, 2.

• Why did the wise men say they came? *(They saw the star; they wanted to worship.)*

But jealous King Herod called the wise men to his court. He wanted all the news about this new star—and future king. With a wicked smile, Herod told the wise men that he, too, wished to worship the new king.

Have children repeat after you. **I wish I may, I wish I might, get the wish I wish tonight!**

But King Herod did not want to share his kingdom. His wishy-washy wish was to do harm to the new king. The wise men listened to Herod's wishful thinking and then went on their way. An evil king would not stop their wish to see the new king. The star moved on and so did they.

One last time have children repeat after you. **I wish I may, I wish I might, get the wish I wish tonight!** Ask a volunteer to read Matthew 2:9–11.

When the star finally stopped over Bethlehem the wise men were joyful. All they needed to do now was look for the place under the bright and special star. They hurried on!

Rise with your children and "travel" over to the bed display. Make sure to take your grab bag with you. **Here is the new king! The wise men bowed and worshiped the true king of the world, Jesus.** Kneel and have your children do the same. **The wise men gave Jesus the precious Christmas presents they had carried so far.** Take the presents from your grab bag and have the children lay them near the bed.

God's purpose in the world is much stronger than any wish. When we wish for something, we hope it will happen, but we don't really know if it will. We don't have to worry about wishing with God. He's the true king, and he does what's best for us—like sending his Son, Jesus, to be our Savior.

Tonight when you look up at the stars, remember that Jesus was born under one very special star so that he could be a Savior to us all. When you receive Christmas presents, remember the presents the wise men brought to worship the child Jesus.

• Why did the wise men give presents to Jesus? *(To worship him.)*
• How can you worship baby Jesus?

Bow heads to pray. **Dear God, we worship with glad hearts our one true king, King Jesus. In his royal name we pray, amen.**

Creamy Faithfulness

On Your Mark

Bible Truth: We devote ourselves to God and make choices to please him.

Bible Verse: "I will give you new hearts. I will give you a new spirit that is faithful to me" (Ezekiel 36:26).

Godprint: Faithfulness

Get Set

Grab Bag: Bible, ice cream sugar cone, 4-inch red satin ball Christmas ornament. Optional: Reproduce the "coupons" from p. 95 and plan a time to serve ice cream cones to kids, such as after the service.

GO!

In a moment I will reach into my grab bag and pull out something that people enjoy eating—especially when topped with a mound of frozen sweetness. When you see it, shout out the first word that comes to mind. Ready?

Reach into your grab bag and hold up the sugar cone. Pause for your kids to shout "ice cream." Yes, that's it! A single, double or even a triple dip scoop would fit nicely on top of this cone. A triple dip peppermint-almond-fudge with rainbow sprinkles would be my top choice! That would look very Christmasy, wouldn't it?

• What is your favorite ice cream flavor?
• What other treats do you like to eat at Christmas time?

I have one more surprise for you. Place the ice cream cone in your lap and reach into your grab bag. **This is not something you eat but something we use when the Christmas holiday comes around. Ready?** Pull out the red satin Christmas ball ornament. **What's this?** *(It's a Christmas ball for a Christmas tree.)*

Right! Hold the Christmas ball in one hand and the ice cream cone in another. **What if we were to join these two things to make something completely new and wonderful?** Drop the satin ball on top of the ice cream cone. **Now what do we have?** *(Something that looks like an ice cream cone, but if you glued it together you could hang it as a decoration from the Christmas tree.)*

Read Ezekiel 36:26 from your Bible or ask a volunteer to read.

• What does this verse say God will give us?
• How would a new heart change us?
• Why is Christmas a good time to think about new hearts?

God gives us new hearts (pick up the red satin ball) and new spirits (break a bit off the end of the sugar cone and blow through it). We become new and wonderful creations in him. God promises to put his Spirit inside here (lay a hand on your chest) to help soften our sinful hearts so we'll follow his rules. And when we follow God's rules we show him that we are faithful to him. When Jesus came to earth as a baby, that was the beginning of our new hearts, because God was with us.

Hmm. God with us. That combination beats a peppermint-almond-fudge with sprinkles cone any day! Gather children in prayer. Dear God, give us new hearts and spirits so that we may remain faithful to you always. In Jesus' name, amen.

Before children head back to their seats distribute the "Free Cone!" coupons you cut before church. **Cones all around for being great listeners today!**

Honk If You Love Jesus

On Your Mark

Bible Truth: I can treat others better than myself.

Bible Story: Jesus washes his disciples' feet (John 13:1–17).

Godprint: Humility

Get Set

Grab Bag:Bible, paper slips prepared as described below, hat or toy car large enough to hold paper slips, water spray bottle

On the paper slips write things found on a car that make noise, such as the horn, wheels, engine, windshield wipers, radio, emergency brake, car alarm, etc. Fold and place slips inside the hat or toy car.

GO!

Take the hat or car filled with slips of paper from your grab bag. **Ready, get set, let's go! Inside my hat** (car) **are slips of paper. On each slip is printed something on an S.U.V that makes noise. I'd like you to pull a slip, read what's on it and make that noise. Let's see if we can guess which car part you have printed on your paper.** Elicit the assistance of older children to help the non-readers in your group.

• A squeaky wheel gets a lot of attention. Can a quiet car with a great bumper sticker do the same? Why or why not?

When slips have been read and vocals performed, have the congregation join you in giving children a round of applause. Then ask all your children to become the noisy wheels of the car by moving fists up and around. As children chug, spurt and sputter, shout **Toot! Toot! Sounds like our Sports Humility Vehicle (S.H.V, for short) is ready to travel...** (quickly reach into your grab bag and remove the water bottle; give your "wheels" a spritz of water)...**straight to the car wash!**

Have your S.H.V come to a quick and silent stop. **Another great way to get from one place to another is to walk.** Open your Bible to John 13. **Jesus and his disciples walked a lot. Today's Bible story talks about feet–feet that get a travel wash from Jesus!**

Read John 13:1, 4-5.

• What did Jesus do for his disciples?
• Would it be hard or easy to wash a best friend's feet?

Squeaky-clean toes all around. Jesus performed a humble and loving service to show his friends he loved them.

• What message was Jesus telling his disciples?

You might think that Jesus was too important to have a job like washing other people's feet. But that's exactly why he did it. He wanted his disciples to know he was thinking of them, and not just himself.

Read John 13:14-15.

• What did Jesus tell his disciples to do?
• Does Jesus really mean that all we have to do is wash each other's feet?
• What example does Jesus want us to follow. *(Think of others first. Be humble.)*

Now it's our turn. Jesus wants us to follow his example and think of others first—and to serve them. When we do we will be blessed. Jesus gives us his Word!

• How can you serve your mom or dad after church today?

Now turn to your neighbor and give his or her shoulders a nice rub. Let's put a shine on our Sports Humility Vehicles.

After a moment, ask kids to bow heads in prayer. **Dear God, help us to serve others in love like Jesus did. With his help we can get the job done. In his name, amen.**

A Question of Loyalty

On Your Mark

Bible Truth: God wants us to show our love and commitment to him.

Bible Story: Peter wants to be loyal, but denies Jesus (John 18:17, 18, 25–27).

Godprint: Loyalty

Get Set

Grab bag: Bible, a photo of a loyal pet, a simple bird sock puppet

GO!

Place the sock puppet out of sight for now. **Good morning! Thanks for coming to visit me.** Hold up the picture of your dog or cat—or pet iguana! **This is Rosy** (or use your pet's real name). **Rosy is my best friend and loyal companion. On chilly days she fetches my slippers. Then she skedaddles into the kitchen and mixes up a nice tall mug of hot cocoa with extra whipped cream. Then as I sip away she lies at my feet and keeps my toes warm. Rosy is as loyal as pets come.**

• Do you have a loyal pet?

Jesus wants us to be loyal to him. Does anyone have a loyal rooster as a pet? Pull out "Mr. Cackle," your pet rooster sock puppet. **Can you crow like a rooster?** Cockle-doodle-doo along with your children. **Very good! Now when Mr. Cackle crows, you crow too. Here we go.**

One chilly night soldiers came to arrest Jesus. They dragged him to the palace of the high priest. Men there made fun of Jesus. They hit and spat at him because he told them he was the Son of God. Peter, one of Jesus' disciples, was standing at a fire nearby. He felt sorry for Jesus. But he was afraid to let others know he was Jesus' friend. They might hit and spit on him too.

Open your Bible and read John 18:17, 18. **Poor Peter. He said he did not know Jesus.** Have Mr. Cackle do his thing!

Read John 18:25–27. **Again Peter said, "No. I do not know anyone named Jesus."** Cockle-doodle-doo with your children.

And one more time Peter said, "No, no, I do not know him one tiny bit! How many times do I have to tell you? No, no, NO, I do not know this Jesus!" Crow one last time.

Three times the rooster crowed to remind Peter that he was not loyal to Jesus. Peter was suddenly very, very sorry that he'd been afraid to tell people Jesus was his friend. Curl Mr. Cackle's head into your shoulder. **Peter ran off and cried.**

• Why was Peter afraid to be loyal to Jesus?
• How can we be loyal to Jesus?
• How can we honor God by being loyal to our friends?

After Jesus rose from the dead, he met Peter on a beach and gave him another chance to be loyal. That made Peter—and Mr. Cackle—very happy. Let's try hard to remember not to turn our backs on our best friend, Jesus.

Bow heads in prayer. **Dear God, help us to show you that we love you, even when we're afraid. In Jesus' name, amen.**

You Won't Believe It!

On Your Mark

Bible Truth: Jesus' resurrection gives us hope for the future.

Bible Story: Mary and Peter find the empty tomb (John 20:1–8).

Godprint: Hope

Get Set

Grab Bag: Bible, powerful flashlight, sealed zip-top bag filled with scented cotton balls or small potpourri sachets

You can scent cotton balls with vanilla extract or spritz with a spicy men's cologne.

GO!

Clap your hands if you've had a brother or sister run into your room—all out of breath—and shout, "You'll never guess what I just saw!" And it's such a fantastic, hard-to-believe story you won't believe it!

• What fantastic stories have your brothers or sisters shared with you?

Who remembers the Bible story of Easter? Pause. That's right. It was a dark and stormy afternoon. Jesus died on a cross. Friends wrapped his lifeless body in spices and placed it in a cave tomb. Pass out the scented sachets. Have children close their eyes and take a sniff. Can you smell the spice? After they put Jesus' body in a tomb, his friends went home to try to understand why Jesus had to die. Hand the Bible to a reader in your group. Read John 20:1.

• What did Mary Magdalene find on that dark morning?

Mary Magdalene ran to find Peter. Out of breath she shouted something like, "You'll never guess what I just saw!"

Read John 20:2. Peter did not believe her fantastic, hard-to-believe story. Peter and a friend ran to check it out for themselves. Read John 20:6–8.

• What did the disciples see when they went to the tomb?

The fantastic, hard-to-believe story was true. The cold, dark tomb was empty. Jesus was…alive! He had risen from the dead just as he said he would! Peter was humbled. Suddenly everything made perfect "scents!" Have children take another sniff of their sachets and smell the sweet "morning-fresh" vanilla.

So…in a dark, dark cave (cup your hand to represent a cave) the light of Jesus' hope shone bright! Place the flashlight under your cupped hand. Turn it on. Your hand will glow! Allow your children's hands to glow bright too.

Jesus rose just as he said he would. Remember, God is in control of our lives. He brings good from everything that happens.

Let's pray. Dear God, your Son died so that we might have a wonderful life. We choose to follow and work for him. Amen.

Out With Doubt!

On Your Mark

Bible Truth: Through faith we believe what Jesus says about himself.

Bible Verse: Thomas said to him, "My Lord, my God!" Then Jesus told him, "Because you have seen me, you have believed. Blessed are those who have not seen me but still have believed" (John 20:28, 29).

Godprint: Faith

Get Set

Grab Bag: Bible, a small whiteboard, dry-erase markers, a large picture of a guinea pig, blindfold

GO!

Everything I learned about drawing I learned in kindergarten. I remember opening my new box of crayons and just waiting for the teacher to say, "Draw me a picture!"

• What is your favorite color crayon?
• If you owned a crayon factory what colorful picture would you draw?

Choose a young volunteer from the group.

Thank you _____(fill in child's name) **for being our guinea pig, I mean volunteer, this morning.** Reach into your bag and pull out the picture of the guinea pig. Hand it to your volunteer to hold. Then take out the whiteboard and marker from your grab bag. Place the whiteboard against your chest and hand the marker to an eager child from your group. (If you don't have a whiteboard, you can use paper.) **Please draw a picture of a guinea pig. She has to be beautiful…just like Matilda here. Ready? Oh, wait a moment. I almost forgot.**

Take the blindfold out of the grab bag. Tie it around the eyes of your young artist. **That's better. Ready? Oh, wait a moment. I almost forgot.** Give him or her a complete turn. **Ready? Draw!**

Give the child a minute or two to try to draw—something! Then remove the blindfold. **Well…it looks like we've got most of Matilda, but there do seem to be a few important parts missing…like her head!** Blindfold a few more volunteers to finish Matilda before putting the marker and board aside. **How much easier things would have been for** _____, _____ **and** _____(fill in the names of your helpful volunteers) if I'd never taken out the blindfold from my bag. In today's Bible passage, however, Jesus tells us that even with full eyesight our eyes only tell part of the story. Jesus had risen from the dead, but Thomas wasn't sure he believed it.

Read John 20:26–29 or ask a volunteer to read.

• What did Jesus tell Thomas to do?
• What does Jesus say about people who have not seen him, but still believe? *(They are blessed.)*

Doubting Thomas taught all believers a very important lesson. We don't need our eyes to see the Savior of the world because with the eyes of faith we can *feel* his love, *hear* his words and *see* his face. Close your eyes for a moment and take a peek! Have your children visualize the face of Christ. Can you see the smile of Jesus?

God's Word tells us all about Jesus. God wants us to have faith in him and believe what he has said.

Gather heads and hearts in prayer. Dear God, help us to have faith in your Son, Jesus. May it grow and grow until it fills us up from top to bottom. Amen.

Fish Sticks

Bible Truth: Jesus helps us understand how others feel.

Bible Verse: The other disciples followed in the boat. They were towing the net full of fish. The shore was only about 100 yards away. When they landed, they saw a fire of burning coals. There was fish on it. There was also some bread…Jesus said to them, "Come and have breakfast" (John 21:8, 9, 12).

Godprint: Empathy

Get Set

Grab Bag: Bible, coffee mug, fish-shaped crackers, lunch sack, craft sticks, marker

Fill your favorite coffee mug with fish crackers. Place it in a lunch sack or zip-top bag to keep the fish from falling overboard. Then draw fish eyes on the craft sticks—two marker circles with a dot in the middle, one on either side of the stick.

GO!

- Who makes breakfast at your house?
- What is the best breakfast for a sleep-in Saturday morning?

Just like you and me, the disciples looked forward to a hot breakfast. Fishing on the Sea of Galilee in the early hours of the morning was hard work and the disciples were hungry. Imagine how delighted they were one day to see Jesus on the shore. He had risen from the dead, and now he was cooking breakfast for them. Read John 21:8–10 or have a strong reader help you.

- Jesus knew the disciples needed breakfast. How did he show them he knew? *(He made breakfast!)*
- Do you think Jesus knows what you need?

Pop your lips like a fish if you would like to have breakfast on a beach with Jesus.

Reach into your grab bag and remove the lunch sack. Carefully pull out the coffee mug. **Hmm. Fish for breakfast. Great idea!** Show the children the fish crackers. **Let's give thanks to Jesus first**

before we eat our fish. Offer a brief prayer of thanks or recite this common table prayer, which some of the children may know.

> *Come, Lord Jesus, be our guest,*
> *And let this food to us be blessed, amen.*

Serve children and allow them to munch as they listen. **The risen Jesus gave the disciples things they needed. He cared for their bodies. He also cared for their hearts and feelings.**

• What "comfort 'n' cozy" words are your favorite?
• How can you show other people that you care for their feelings?

The disciples had so much to do now. Spreading the Good News of Jesus would be a happy but hard task. The disciples did not want to go it alone. The disciples were very, very thankful to have Jesus cook, care and love them.

Reach into your grab bag and remove the craft sticks. Distribute them. **This week I'd like you to sit down with your markers and make a fish stick! Not the kind you eat but one you'll use as a bookmarker. Use the craft stick I just gave you to make a very handsome fish with bold, bright stripes and a flashy tail. Two very bright eyes have been done for you.** Point to the eyes on the stick.

Use your fish stick to bookmark John 21 in your Bible. Then the next time your family gathers for a breakfast of hot pancakes or eggs and biscuits...go fish! Remember that Jesus said, "Come and have breakfast" because he cared about his disciples. Read how a breakfast on the beach story is really a love story from Jesus to his disciples...and you. Then think of a way to show your family that you care. Cleaning up would make a great start!

Bow for prayer. **Dear Jesus, thank you for understanding how we feel. Help us to understand how other people feel and help them to know you better. In your name, amen.**

Spirit Wind

On Your Mark

Bible Truth: God gives us his Holy Spirit to help us tell others about Jesus.

Bible Story: Suddenly a sound came from heaven. It was like a strong wind blowing. It filled the whole house where they were sitting (Acts 2:2).

Godprint: Evangelism

Get Set

Grab Bag: Bible, three balloons, three pony beads, colorful feathers, poster board

Ahead of time, push a pony bead inside each of the deflated balloons. Allow the bead to drop to the bottom of the balloon before blowing it up. Knot inflated balloons and drop them in your grab bag. Finally, print in bold letters, "The Holy Spirit Lives in Me!" on poster board.

GO!

I have a super-special, top secret message to share. And because our ears sometimes work better with our eyes closed, go ahead and close your eyes! Pause. Shh! Listen carefully now as I whisper the super-special message to_____(fill in a child's name). Once you hear the message you may open your eyes to pass it along. You'll know it's your turn when you feel your ear tickle! Whisper the following: *"The Holy Spirit lives in me!"* Have the message travel in one ear and out the other. While children whisper away, hold up the sign with the message printed for the congregation to see. Put the sign away before you request the last child in the group to turn to the congregation and shout the message out loud.

Very close! I think we got all of the important words. In today's Scripture we hear of the day the Holy Spirit blew like a breath of fresh air into the lives of Christians.

Have a reader open the Bible and read Acts 2:1. We're gathered here much like the believers were on that day.

Read Acts 2:2. Wow. A strong wind! Take out the three balloons from the bag and throw them out to your group. If you have a balloon, shake it. Pause as children shake the balloons. Now hold the balloons up to your neighbor's ear and—ssh!—so that they can hear the rush and roar

of a strong wind! The swirling pony bead inside the balloons will sound like the rise and fall of "a violent wind." After all your children have had the chance to hear the wind, have them carry the balloons out into the congregation so they, too, can give a shake and a listen.

Read Acts 2:3, 4.

• What happened to the believers that day? *(They were filled with the Spirit and spoke in languages they did not know.)*

The Bible says "tongues of fire" settled on the believers. Let's put some tongues of fire on our heads too. Reach into your grab bag and remove the feathers. Distribute them and have children stick them into their hair, if possible, so that the feathers stand up.

Just as your feathers are many colors, the believers spoke many different languages that day.

• Do you know someone who speaks another language?
• Can you imagine what it would be like to suddenly speak a language you did not know?
• Why was it important for the believers to speak so many languages?

The answer is super-special—but not at all top-secret. God poured out his Spirit onto the believers so they could tell the world about the salvation and life-saving message of Jesus, the Savior. Everybody there heard about Jesus in words they could understand. God sent the Holy Spirit so we would know that he is always there to help us tell others about Jesus.

Let's pray now and thank God for the Holy Spirit, who helps us tell others about Jesus. Bow heads for prayer. **Dear God, thank you for sending your Holy Spirit to live in us. Help us to always listen to what your Holy Spirit says. Amen.**

Have children remove the feathers from their hair and place them inside your grab bag before returning to their seats.

Butterfly Pin

On Your Mark

Bible Truth: God wants us to turn away from sin and follow him.

Bible Verse: I have come so they can have life. I want them to have it in the fullest possible way (John 10:10b).

Godprint: Repentance

Get Set

Grab Bag: Bible, "pinch" clothespins

Reproduce the butterflies on p. 110 and cut them apart. A few days before your sermon, gather any budding artists in your congregation and color in the butterflies.

GO!

Easter often makes us think of springtime and the new life that comes to the world in the spring. Flowers, trees, butterflies—we see new life in lots of ways. Sometimes we use a butterfly as a picture of new life. Jesus was in a dark tomb and then he burst out of it the way a beautiful butterfly bursts out of the caterpillar's cocoon. At Easter we celebrate that Jesus is wonderfully alive!

• If Jesus were really a butterfly, what pretty colors do you think he'd be?

Take the pretty paper butterflies from your grab bag and distribute them. Save one for yourself. **Beautiful butterflies! Here's how to make them fly. Make your fingers into a pair of make-believe scissors like this** (demonstrate for your children) **and slide your Easter butterfly in between. Now "point and wave" your fingers to make the butterfly wings flap up and down. While you wave, say, Jesus is alive!** Pause for children to wave their butterflies and respond.

Look at your butterfly and say, **Sadly, many of us forget all about Jesus the day *after* Easter. Instead of showing the world that he is alive in us we flutter back to our old sinful ways.** Take the clothespins from your grab bag and distribute them.

• What hurtful things do we do that keep others from seeing Jesus in us?

As children mention hurts and selfish actions, have them attach their clothespins to your butterfly. Depending on the size of your group, everyone may not be able to participate. Hold up the heavy-burdened butterfly for everyone to see, then let it drop to the floor. **With so much weight a beautiful butterfly cannot fly. It can't beat its wings. It can't soar free.** Open your Bible and read the second part of John 10:10.

• What did Jesus say he came for? *(To give life.)*
• How is having new life in Jesus a wonderful, happy thing?
• How can we turn away from sin and follow God after Easter?

With each response have children who didn't place clothespins on the butterfly come up and remove the clothespins. Place your Easter butterfly once again between your fingers. Flap and fly right!

Jesus came to earth from his Father's heavenly home to live among us, to die among us and then to rise from the dead to save us from the heaviness of our sins. He wants us to have life in the fullest possible way. He doesn't want us burdened down by our sins.

Tomorrow and all the days after Easter, remember to turn away from sin and fly in the light of Jesus' love and life. Jesus is alive! And in him now so are we.

Bow heads in prayer. **Dear God, thank you for the life we have in Jesus. He has risen! Amen.**

Index of Godprints and Topics

Index of Scripture References